The Collected Works of
William Howard Taft

The Collected Works of
William Howard Taft

David H. Burton, General Editor

VOLUME VI

THE PRESIDENT AND HIS POWERS

AND

THE UNITED STATES AND PEACE

Edited with Commentary by
W. Carey McWilliams and Frank X. Gerrity

OHIO UNIVERSITY PRESS

ATHENS

Ohio University Press, Athens, Ohio 45701
© 2003 by Ohio University Press
Printed in the United States of America
All rights reserved

Ohio University Press books are printed on acid-free paper ⊗ ™

12 11 10 09 08 07 06 05 04 03   5 4 3 2 1

The President and His Powers, originally published under the title *Our Chief Magistrate and His Powers,*
is based on the Columbia University Lectures, under the George Blumenthal Foundation, delivered
in 1915. Copyright 1916 by Columbia University Press.
The United States and Peace, copyright 1914 by Charles Scribner's Sons. First printed May 1914.

Publication of *The Collected Works of William Howard Taft* has been made possible in part through the
generous support of the Earhart Foundation of Ann Arbor, Michigan, and the Louisa Taft Semple
Foundation of Cincinnati, Ohio.

Photograph of William Howard Taft courtesy of William Howard Taft National Historic Site.

Library of Congress Cataloging-in-Publication Data
(Revised for volume 6)

Taft, William H. (William Howard), 1857–1930.
The President and his powers ; and, The United States and peace /
edited with commentary by W. Carey McWilliams and Frank X. Gerrity.
p.   cm. — (The collected works of William Howard Taft ; v. 6)
ISBN 0-8214-1500-X (cloth)
1. Presidents—United States.   2. Executive power—United States.   3.
Monroe doctrine.   4. Arbitration, International.   I. McWilliams, Wilson
C.   II. Gerrity, Frank X., 1923–2001.   III. Taft, William H. (William
Howard), 1857–1930.   United States and peace.   IV. Title: United States
and peace.   V. Title.
E660 .T11   2001 vol. 6
[JK516]
352.23'5'0973—dc21   2003045956

Dedicated to
the Taft family,
for five generations serving
Ohio and the nation

The Collected Works of
William Howard Taft

David H. Burton, General Editor

VOLUME ONE
Four Aspects of Civic Duty and *Present Day Problems*
Edited with commentary by David H. Burton and A. E. Campbell

VOLUME TWO
Political Issues and Outlooks
Edited with commentary by David H. Burton

VOLUME THREE
Presidential Addresses and State Papers
Edited with commentary by David H. Burton

VOLUME FOUR
Presidential Messages to Congress
Edited with commentary by David H. Burton

VOLUME FIVE
Popular Government and *The Anti-trust Act and the Supreme Court*
Edited with commentary by David Potash and Donald F. Anderson

VOLUME SIX
The President and His Powers and *The United States and Peace*
Edited with commentary by W. Carey McWilliams and Frank X. Gerrity

VOLUME SEVEN
Taft Papers on League of Nations
Edited with commentary by Frank X. Gerrity

VOLUME EIGHT
"Liberty under Law" and Selected Supreme Court Opinions
Edited with commentary by Francis Graham Lee
Cumulative Index

Contents

THE PRESIDENT AND
HIS POWERS

The President and His Powers

Commentary

W. Carey McWilliams

*T*he President and His Powers is a grand book, unique among the reflections of former presidents. Taft draws on his experience in the presidency and in the executive branch, and he speaks to many of the political issues of his time—most obviously, his disagreement with Theodore Roosevelt's "stewardship" theory of presidential power. But his argument is more than a polemic or a memoir. In the best sense of the word, Taft's book is theoretical, concerned with the nature of executive power and its place in the American system.

Taft's writing is suited to that design. His prose is Olympian; clear but stately, a little ponderous but remarkably balanced. He makes his case against Roosevelt's doctrine without rancor and in terms of principle, as if indicating that the issues involved transcend personalities. Of course, Taft cannot resist the wry aside that TR's identification of himself with Lincoln "might otherwise have escaped notice," given the differences, "presumably superficial," between the two, but Taft's humor is often directed against himself. The sly quality of his wit—a good many lines are delivered with the literary equivalent of a wink or raised eyebrow—hints at the subtler dimensions and subtexts of his thought. And his insistence that an executive needs a sense of humor prescribes a measure of amused observation, a philosopher's appreciation for the comic side of human politics.

Perhaps Taft had too much of that sensibility to be a great president. Certainly, political scientists think so. Almost without exception, they rank him as a good administrator, but a mediocre chief executive. James McGregor Burns was comparatively generous in rating Taft as "average," along with John Quincy Adams, Martin Van Buren, Chester Arthur, Benjamin Harrison, William McKinley, and Herbert Hoover, some good company, but hardly a collection of all-stars. Clinton Rossiter had positive things to say about Taft's technical competence, but grouped him with McKinley and Coolidge as representatives of a conservatism inferior to that of Eisenhower. And Stephen Skowronek, perhaps the most distinguished contemporary student of the presidency, referred to Taft's term as a "debacle."

Some of this is unfair and more of it rests on Taft's lack of sympathy for the activist theory of the presidency that has come to dominate political science. In the intellectual arena, so far, Theodore Roosevelt's view or variations on it have won most of the laurels, relegating Taft to a "symbol of standpattism" if not political apostasy. In part, this is a caricature: Taft, no reactionary, was a conservative progressive, hostile to organized labor but also suspicious of big business, a more effective "trust-buster" than TR and able to point to a record of significant reform. (In fact, Taft's "ultimate act of betrayal," in Theodore Roosevelt's view, lay in his insistence on pressing an antitrust case against U.S. Steel, rejecting TR's distinction between "constructive" and "destructive" trusts in favor of a strict adherence to the law.)

As president, Stephen Skowronek indicates, Taft inherited an impossible task. Theodore Roosevelt's administration, by strengthening and legitimating progressives, had upset the old political balance. Taft honorably tried to follow TR in seeking reforms through existing institutions, only to discover that the center would not hold.

That Taft did not see as much indicates the extent to which he lacked the gift and the disposition for politics. Amiable, conflict-averse, often candid to a fault, he was not ruled by the great passions of democratic politics: ambition, the yearning for public favor, and the desire for revenge. Hampered by his rectitude, his concern for accuracy, and his devotion to the law, Taft was almost bound to be politically maladroit. His addresses, James David Barber writes, sacrificed "eloquence for accuracy. . . . He delivered an opinion when he might have preached a sermon." Even his brother gave him low marks in the arts of politics.

But the very qualities that limited Taft's success as president and in the practice of politics commend him as a *student* of the presidency. Temperamentally unsuited to be an advocate, he was superbly fitted to be a judge, looking beyond partisan claims in the effort to discern governing principles. His writing does not often scintillate, but his intellectual craftsmanship is deft, marked by evidence of learning and often by genuine profundity. Even Taft's critics respect his arguments and his scholarship: for example, Harold Laski, Taft's polar opposite ideologically, approvingly cited Taft's views on the president's term, on relations between the executive and Congress, and on the veto power.

And Clinton Rossiter referred to Taft's opinion in *Myers v. U.S.* as "breath-taking." Intellectually, Taft reached beyond practice toward theory, a quality of mind evident in the subtleties of *The President and His Powers.*

Taft's argument turns on his disagreement with Theodore Roosevelt regarding presidential power: Taft insists that all presidential power must be "fairly and reasonably traced to some specific grant of power or justly implied or included within such express grant as proper and necessary to its exercise"; the president has no "undefined residuum of power" to act for the public good. By contrast, TR held that the president is the "steward of the people," limited in his power to act for the common good *only* by some express provision of the Constitution, an "advocacy of the higher law and his obligation to execute it," Taft wrote, "which is a little startling in a constitutional republic."

Beneath this apparent contestation—Roosevelt for a plenary view of executive power, Taft for a more limited one—is a significant agreement on fundamentals: like Roosevelt's doctrine of "stewardship," Taft's view of the president as "Chief Agent" of the people presumes that the executive is "representative," charged with carrying out the people's will, rightly understood.

But they differ, crucially, in their view of law. Roosevelt saw the law primarily as a *restraint* on power *derived from* public opinion; for Taft, the law *empowers* the president precisely because it conveys a *claim on* public opinion. In that sense, in Taft's theory, the presidency is potentially *stronger* than it is in TR's terms, since it encourages a president who is psychologically more autonomous, less dependent on public sentiment, and more able to set his or her own course.

And in fact, while Taft insists that every presidential power be traceable to a specific grant of power, he construes those provisions very generously, affording the president a broad imperium. He allows the president virtually complete control over the executive branch, for example, including the power to interpret statutes—often outside any potential judicial scrutiny, so that such administrative applications determine the effective meaning of the law. This extends to a vaulting definition of executive privilege. Congress, Taft argues, cannot elicit "confidential information" if the president "does not deem the disclosure . . . prudent or in the public interest." Similarly, Taft contends that to subpoena the president as a witness "would interfere with his public duties," and that while in office the president may be "beyond the compulsory processes" of the courts. Evidently, the contemporary Supreme Court has afforded the executive much less protection; Taft's position, if adopted, would have allowed President Clinton to avoid testifying in the Jones case, possibly sparing the country the tragicomedy of impeachment.

Similarly, Taft argues that the president's duty to see the laws executed confers power which is "inferable" from the "general code of duties under the laws," though nowhere made explicit, rehearsing the bizarre story behind *In Re Neagle* and agreeing with the Court's discovery in that case of inherent executive power "implied by the nature of government under the Constitution." Similarly, Taft indicates that the president's powers as Commander-in-Chief effectively convey an authority "quite beyond his power under the Constitution directly to effect," just as the president's powers in foreign affairs extend well beyond ordinary constitutional or statutory limits.

Moreover, beyond the president's formal powers, Taft saw a need and title for symbolic leadership, including the direction of national opinion. The president, he wrote, is the "personal embodiment and representative" of the "dignity and majesty" of the people, an appropriate spokesperson for the country as a whole. Approving Wilson's decision to deliver his messages to Congress in person as a way to focus "the attention of the country," Taft gave a measure of support to the development of the "rhetorical presidency"—the president conceived as a manager of public opinion.

Loving the Constitution and the laws, Taft was no less devoted to the theory that underlies both. Like the framers, Taft saw the laws as conventions, contrivances rooted in contract, a fenced area of order surrounded by a fundamentally lawless nature. The rule of law requires protecting this space against invasions and disruptions which are external to law and only partly subject to its control. A constitutional regime, consequently, must include some power—Locke had called it "prerogative"—capable of responding to such challenges and changes on their own terms. Almost necessarily, that power belongs to the principate, especially in the modern world, where new forces are ever more threatening and transformations ever more rapid. In these terms, while the presidency is created *by* law, the president's duties leave her or him with one foot *outside* the law. Restrictions on presidential power, Taft wrote, are themselves limited by the need for "discretion and promptness" in pursuing the public good in "times of emergency or legislative neglect or inaction."

It was precisely because Taft recognized that presidential power is, in so many ways, illimitable in *content* that he insisted on limits in *form,* demanding that the president appeal to the specific provisions of the Constitution, the imperatives of action acknowledging the moral authority of words. As a champion of the rule of law—it was his desire to subordinate private power *to* law that made him a progressive, just as his insistence that public power respect law made him a conservative—Taft was concerned to maintain the supremacy of law in *principle* the more it seemed questionable in practice.

Taft begins his book by emphasizing the Constitution's forms, reminding his readers that the separation of powers is more strictly defined here than it had been in Britain. But immediately, he indicates that the Constitution's separation of powers is much less clear than Montesquieu's. Theory informs American law, but yields ground to practice. Executive power, especially, eludes firm definition by "treatises" or "judicial decisions," reaching beyond the effective authority of courts and laws. In fact, Taft goes on to observe, the line between what is subject to judicial control and what is not "offers an opportunity for the study of nice distinctions which I shall not, for lack of space, further pursue." Yet surely this "nice" distinction is *crucial,* particularly for a thinker like Taft who stresses the forms. Is his reluctance to pursue the question really to be explained by lack of space? Or is it that, pushed to the limit, the argument would point to the extent that all judicial power, all constitutional government, and certainly all limits on executive power finally depend on political judgment?

At decisive points, Taft indicates, any restraint on the executive depends on political institutions (the courts not included) and on the people as "ultimate sovereign." As that suggests, constitutional government relies on the education of citizens, a pedagogy in which the president has a vital role. Taft's own title for the book speaks of the president as chief *magistrate* precisely because he wanted to underline the president's responsibilities as a teacher, by word and conduct influencing the public's understanding of and respect for constitutional life.

He is counseling both presidents and citizens, for example, when he comments that, while opposition from Congress is often irksome, it is also *useful*. The "bane of political methods," Taft argues, is the "overwhelming mass of ill-digested legislation," so that a "respite" has considerable value. Strikingly, Taft's language echoes that of the Antifederalist Cato, who observed that a democracy should be "well-digested," its laws thoroughly assimilated to habit and opinion. Taft's position indicates a similar concern for law that has become internalized, enforced not in the courts but in the souls of citizens. The great test of republican government, in fact, lies in its ability to develop a public that accepts the law's constraints and forms as rightful restraints on its own will. That challenge also marks, for Taft, the measure of a president: since the people are inclined to hold presidents accountable for all sins "of omission and commission," they create a tendency to expand authority, pushing and tempting executives to seek power as unlimited as their responsibility. The truly great presidents, Taft suggests, are those who resist that temptation, reminding the people that their capacity for self-government, and hence their dignity, depends on a government of forms and laws.

1

Distribution of Governmental Powers

The Veto Power

The framers of our Constitution were much affected by Montesquieu's appreciation of the English Constitution and his insistence upon a division of the government into Legislative, Executive and Judicial branches and a separation of one from the other, as the best security for civil liberty. They, thus, made this division and separation more clearly marked and rigid than in the British Constitution. In a way that I shall attempt to *describe* later, there was established the power of the Judicial branch, by its decisions in litigated cases, to construe the limitations on the Executive and Legislative powers contained in the Constitution and thereby through the moral influence and force of its judgments to affect the future action of the Executive and the Congress, and restrain them within the limits of the fundamental law as declared by it. But these judgments of the Supreme Court can only be rendered in actual and litigated cases, in which one individual has sued another and in which generally some constitutional right of an individual is infringed by Legislative or Executive action. There is in the scope of the jurisdiction of both the Executive and Congress a wide field of action in which individual rights are not affected in such a way that they can be asserted and vindicated in a court. In this field, the construction of the power of each branch and its limitations must be left to itself and the political determination of the people who are the ultimate sovereign asserting themselves at the polls. Precedents from previous administrations and from previous Congresses create an historical construction of the extent and limitations of their respective powers, aided by the discussions arising in a conflict of jurisdictions between them. The field of action by the Executive is perhaps less subject to judicial interpretation than that of Congress. Most legislation of doubtful validity in one way or another ultimately comes before the Court. And so the limitations of Congress may be much more fully studied in the Supreme Court Reports than those of Executive action. This makes the definition of Executive power somewhat more difficult, and somewhat less within the usually trodden path of students of constitutional law, than that of Congress. By actual experience in the exercise of Executive power, one must acquire some familiarity with precedents not set forth in treatises and not elaborately and carefully discussed in judicial decisions. In the necessary paucity of living ex-Presidents, therefore, my empirical knowledge of the extent and limits of our national Executive power makes me venture to ask your attention to the subject of these chapters.

The question of the Presidency, its duties, its responsibilities and its limitations, ought perhaps to be settled not in the heat of the issues that constantly arise for the decision of the incumbent, but rather in the careful study from an unbiased standpoint of the *historian and the jurist*. Still no such determination will be a fair one that does not give some weight to the practical considerations that crowd upon one charged with executive responsibility. I may add, on the other hand, that retirement from office to a place of study and contemplation, rather than of action, modifies somewhat the views formed, *dum fervet opus*. This, I think, is significant of the value of having, from time to time, the constitutional limitations upon the Executive power interpreted by another branch of the government than that to whose action they apply.

The inefficient performance of their executive functions by the Continental Congress and the ad interim committee of that Congress, no one can doubt who will read the correspondence of Washington during the Revolution, or observe the stagnant chaos there was after independence was won. The example of the one-man power under George III, which he maintained by his corrupt control of Parliament, made the Convention doubtful as to the methods by which, and the persons through whom, the Executive power should be exercised. Roger Sherman, representing a minority, thought that the Executive should be the mere agent of the Legislature to carry out their will, and others thought that the Executive should not only thus be controlled, but in order to protect against abuse of powers, it should be vested in a number of persons. Randolph of Virginia is understood to have supported this view. Hamilton, at the other extreme, thought that the Executive should be single, should be elected for life, and should be given ample powers independent of the Legislative branch and absolute power to veto its enactments. The happy result which was reached between the two extremes is only one of the many instances of the triumph of clear-headed common sense, wise patriotism and the personal sacrifice of cherished notions, which we find in the compromises embodied in our wonderful Constitution.

The result in respect of the Executive, as you know, was that the President was to be elected for a term of four years, by an electoral college elected by the people of the states, or in such manner as the legislature of each state might provide, and was given wide powers, not rigidly limited, including the power of qualified veto, under which he could prevent any bill from becoming law unless it could subsequently be passed over his veto by a two-thirds vote in each House of Congress.

I am strongly inclined to the view that it would have been a wiser provision, as it was at one time voted in the Convention, to make the term of the President six or seven years, and render him ineligible thereafter. Such a change would give to the Executive greater courage and independence in the discharge of his duties. The absorbing and diverting interest in the reëlection of the incumbent, taken by those Federal civil servants who regard their own tenure as dependent upon his, would disappear and the efficiency of administration in the last eighteen months of a term would be maintained.

I think, too, it would have been better to bring the Executive a little closer in touch with Congress in the initiation of legislation and its discussion, notably in the matter of budgets and the economical administration of governmental affairs. The great problem that is forcing itself upon the attention of the American people is the method of restraining the extravagance of legislatures and of Congresses. The people themselves are largely to blame for this, not the people as the whole, but the people divided into districts, because the constituencies of members of Congress and of Senators stimulate their representatives in a competitive effort to get as much money out of the public treasury for their respective districts as possible, and are prone to decline reëlecting representatives who fail in this contest. I have not time to dwell on the enormous burden that this selfishness of the people of each district and of their representative imposes upon the government and upon all the people. The waste of money in river and harbor bills, in public building bills, in the establishment of army posts and of navy yards at places selected, not because they are most useful to the army and navy in the economic administration of military and naval defenses, but because they are in favored districts, have had much to do with the increase by leaps and bounds of our actual governmental expenditure. Every other government but ours has what is called a budget system. It was best developed perhaps in the English system of government, and its historical growth is interesting to trace and is useful in order to point the way to the curbing of legislative extravagance. I do not mean to say that the heads of bureaus and even the heads of departments in the Executive branch may not be prone to extravagance, but the result of my experience, which I am sure is borne out by the conclusion of others, is that the Chief Executive, because he is the one whose method of choice and whose range of duties have direct relation to the people as a whole and the government as a whole, is most likely to feel the necessity for economy in total expenditures. It is true of the governor of a state, as it is of the President of the United States. Those who are least moved by anxiety as to the totals are the members of the Legislative branch who are struggling to get as much money as they can out of the general treasury for their respective local constituencies.

In English history, the King and his Ministers ran the government, and the early struggle of Parliament was to restrain the King. The Commons of England by hard effort finally confirmed to themselves the power to refuse to the King money which he asked to carry on the government of the Kingdom. He came before them and said, "I need and request this much money to discharge the duties of the Crown," and the Commons scrutinized his demands, and frequently in the giving exacted from him conditions and limitations. More than two centuries ago, in the government that thus grew up, there was adopted a rule in Parliament that no member could be heard to move for an increase in the supplies and none would be granted unless asked by the Crown. In other words, the Crown was asking the Commons for money, and the function of the Commons was to examine the merit of the request and to cut down from the supplies asked, without power to increase them. The due course at the present day is for the Crown through its Ministers and Parliament to submit for discussion the supplies that each department of the government needs, to have such supplies voted by Parliament, without any increase. After the supplies have been voted, it becomes the duty of the Ministers of the Crown to propose to Parliament through the Chancellor of the Exchequer the budget, that is, a statement of the total proposed expenditure and of the means by which the revenue is to be raised with which to meet the cost. In this way the extravagance on the part of Parliament is avoided, and the government takes over the responsibility for economy and efficiency in government. Of course Parliament has the general legislative power, and it may pass laws imposing upon the Crown new duties of administration requiring the appropriation of additional funds to discharge these new duties. The Crown must submit an estimate for this increase. I have been perhaps more detailed in this statement than I ought to have been in this connection, for the reason that your late Constitutional Convention has grappled with the question and attempted to solve it in the proposed amendments to your Constitution upon this head. It is one of the most important steps of progress that has been taken in constitutional law in this country. In all the wild fads and nostrums that we find set forth in recent constitutional amendments adopted in various states, this stands out as a shining light of hope and a vindication of optimism. If New York succeeds in adopting this system, by which the governor submits estimates and a budget of expenditures and proposed revenues, and the legislature of New York is forbidden to increase the estimates by him submitted, the alarming expenditure and extravagance of government expenses will be halted, and this without in any degree reducing the proper legislative control of the general scope and extent of governmental action and expenditure. Upon the governor and those associated with him will be placed the responsibility for running that government which the legislature has provided by law, as efficiently and economically as it can be done, and the inconsiderate selfishness of local constituencies will be defeated. Success of this system in New York will, I doubt not, lead to a similar reform in the government at Washington. Now not only is Congress unlimited in its extravagance, due to the selfishness of the different congressional constituencies, but Congress as a whole and each House as a unit have by committee government deliberately parted with any actual efficient control of the total annual expenditures from the public treasury. Nor has Congress earnestly cooperated in the past with the Executive in efforts to secure a more economical organization of the government and the elimination of duplication of functions and greater saving and efficiency in the departments. I think, therefore, that our Federal Constitution might be improved in imposing the duty of framing a budget on the Executive and limiting the power of Congress in the voting of appropriations, so that it may give all that the Executive asks to run the government as organized by Congress through general laws, and may not have the specific power to increase the appropriations which the Executive says on his oath and his responsibility are enough to carry on the government duly established by Congress.

As every President has to do, I made many addresses, and the gentleman who introduced me, by way of exalting the occasion rather than the guest, not infrequently said that he was about to introduce one who exercised greater governmental power than any monarch in Europe. I need hardly point out the inaccuracies of this remark, by comparing the powers of the President of the United States with those of the rulers of countries in which there is not real popular legislative control. The powers of the German Emperor, of the Emperor of Austria, and the Emperor of Russia are far wider than those of the President of the United States, although there are in each of those countries legislative bodies with members more or less representative of the people, with some power of governmental control. On the other hand, in really parliamentary governments, the head of the state is less powerful than our President. In England, as it is, the King reigns, but does not govern, and the same thing is true in the Dominion of Canada, of the Governor-General. In France, the President presides, but does not govern. In such parliamentary governments, however, there is a real ruler who exercises in some important respects a greater power than the President of the United States. He is the leader of the majority in the popular house and remains in office only as long as he has that majority behind him. He is the premier, and exercises both executive and legislative functions. The executive head of the state, whether King or President or Governor-General, follows his recommendation in executive work, and he with his colleagues in the Cabinet, as responsible Ministers so-called, controls the legislation.

It would be idle to discuss which is the better form of government. It may be generally said that those who have a parliamentary or responsible government, as it is called, like that form, and that we like our form. Ours is more rigid, in that it divides the Executive from the Legislative, but is like parliamentary government in that in both the Judicial branch is independent of the other two. It is often said that parliamentary government is more responsive to the will of the people than ours in which we have the rigid system of an election of the President every four years and of a Congress every two years; whereas whenever public opinion changes in a parliamentary or responsible form of government, the government changes accordingly. This is hardly accurate. The parliamentary government is responsive to the views of the majority of the members of the more popular house, and if those views do not change, and that majority continues to support the existing Ministers of the Crown who have been selected from its members, the government will last as long as the law permits it to last. Until recently the period was seven years in England and is now five years. This majority in the popular house, the House of Commons, is always elected in a bitter political controversy and the members of the majority are always elected as political partisans. They and not the people must change their views if the political character of the government is to change.

It is true, that when a government in England gets its power from a majority in the House of Commons, made up not of all the members of one party, but of the members of one party, united with those of smaller groups of members representing a class or special interest, then changes in the parliamentary management are likely to be more frequent. In the present Parliament, there is the Liberal Party, the Irish Party and the Labor Party. The two latter are groups, small in number as compared with the Liberal Party, but needed in making up the Ministers' majority. This gives the groups holding the balance of power an opportunity to force measures in their special interest, that as separate issues might not be approved by a majority of Parliament or of the voters of the Kingdom, a condition which is not conducive to the best considered legislation.

It is true that a parliamentary government offers an opportunity for greater effectiveness in that the same mind or minds control the executive and the legislative action, and the one can be closely suited to the other; whereas our President has no initiative in respect to legislation given him by law except that of mere recommendation, and no method of entering into the argument and discussion of the proposed legislation while pending in Congress, except that of a formal message or address. To one charged with the responsibilities of the President, especially where he has party pledges to perform, this seems a defect, but whatever I thought while in office, I am inclined now to think that the defect is more theoretical than actual. It usually happens that the party which is successful in electing a President is also successful in electing a Congress to sustain him. The natural party cohesion and loyalty, and a certain power and prestige which the President has when he enters office, make his first Congress one in which he can exercise much influence in the framing and passage of legislation to fulfil party promises. The history of the present administration and that of many administrations bear me out in this. But it is said that not infrequently the second Congress of an administration contains a majority politically adverse to the President in either one or both of its Houses which makes affirmative legislation impossible and limits congressional action to appropriation bills and non-political measures, if there are any such. The President in such a case naturally chafes under his inability to put through important bills, which he deems of the highest value. On the whole, however, I do not think the country suffers from this in an age and generation when the bane of political methods, and the danger to the best interests of the country, is in the overwhelming mass of ill-digested legislation. We live in a stage of politics, where legislators seem to regard the passage of laws as much more important than the results of their enforcement. The value of the legislation seems not to be in the good of its operation, but in its vote-getting quality, and its use as molasses for the catching of political flies. Therefore, a system in which we may have an enforced rest from legislation for two years is not bad. It affords an opportunity for proper digestion of recent legislation and for the detection of its defects.

Real progress in government must be by slow stages. Radical and revolutionary changes, arbitrarily put into operation, are not likely to be permanent or to accomplish the good which is prophesied of them. My observation of new reform legislation of a meritorious character is that Congress and its members must be educated up to its value by those who have studied it and become convinced of its wisdom. It will be found that much of the good legislation that has gone on to the statute book has been pending before successive sessions of Congress and successive Congresses until Congress and the public have become familiar with the reasons for its adoption, until discussions lasting over from one Congress to another have subjected the proposals to useful scrutiny and amendment, and until it thus acquires a form that Congress is willing to adopt. Sessions therefore at which legislation is not finally adopted, in which there is much discussion of proposed legislation, may often be most useful to the public, both in defeating legislation which ought not to be enacted and in framing for future adoption legislation which will be useful. The provision in some legislatures, Massachusetts especially, that every bill which is introduced must be considered or defeated or passed is not in my judgment a useful provision. It is apt to give unripe laws by forcing undigested and premature expression of opinion in the votes of legislators. Bars in music are used in the maintenance of harmony, and contribute to the comfort of the auditor. The world is not going to be saved by legislation, and is really benefited by an occasional two years of respite from the panacea and magic that many modern schools of politicians seem to think are to be found in the words, "Be it enacted."

The President has both legislative and executive power. Among his executive functions we shall find those which are purely executive and those which are quasi-legislative and are quasi-judicial.

The character of the veto power is purely legislative. The Constitution provides that after both Houses shall have passed a bill, it shall be presented to the President; that if he approve it, he shall sign it, but, if not, that he shall return it, with his objection, to the House in which it originated, which shall proceed to reconsider it; and that if two-thirds of the House agree to pass the bill, it shall be sent with the objections of the President to the other House, where it shall be reconsidered, and if approved by two-thirds of that House, it shall become a law.

It has been suggested by some that the veto power is executive. I do not quite see how. Of course the President has no power to introduce a bill into either House. He has the power of recommending such measures as he shall judge necessary and expedient to the consideration of Congress. But he takes no part in the running discussion of the bill after it is introduced or in its amendments. He has no power to veto parts of the bill and allow the rest to become a law. He must accept it or reject it, and his rejection of it is not final unless he can find one more than one-third of one of the Houses to sustain him in his veto. But even with these qualifications, he is still a participant in the legislation. Except for his natural and proper anxiety not to oppose the will of the two great legislative bodies, and to have harmony in the government, the reasons which control his action must be much like those which affect the action of the members of Congress.

A discussion of the veto power by Mr. Edward Campbell Mason, in a Harvard publication, gives an interesting view of its origin. The author expresses the opinion that the veto is the result of the shrinking of what was once a broad affirmative legislative function of the King. He says that in early days laws were enacted on a petition of Parliament to the King, asking for legislation, and that the law became effective by the King's proclamation declaring the law as he wished it to be. For a long period the King did not confine himself to the request of Parliament in their petition; but on the occasion of each request through his proclamation exercised the affirmative power of formulating laws. As Parliament acquired greater influence they resented the King's proclaiming something different from that which they requested. They therefore presented to the King the proposed statute drawn in proper and exact terms and successfully resisted his giving it new form and substance. He was thereafter required to proclaim the legislation as requested or veto it. His function in legislation thus became one of negation only. It has been contended that the President may not exercise the veto power except when the bill presented to him is unconstitutional. Such a view of his duty is supposed to find color of support in a proposal made and strongly advocated in the Constitutional Convention. It provided for the revision of bills which had passed both Houses by a Council, to include the President and the Supreme Judges, with the power to reject bills which had passed both Houses when they transgressed the

constitutional limits of Congressional discretion. It cannot be said, however, that the provision for the Executive veto as adopted in the Constitution implies any such limitation. It is true that the power is one of negation
only, but the history of its origin shows that even in its qualified form, it
is legislative in its nature, a brake rather than a steam chest, but nevertheless
a very important part of the machinery for making laws. The Constitution
makes the President's veto turn on the question whether he approves the
bill or not. The term "approve" is much too broad to be given the narrow
construction by which it shall only authorize the President to withhold his
signature when the reason for his disapproval of the bill is its invalidity.
No better word could be found in the language to embrace the idea of
passing on the merits of the bill. If anything has been established by actual
precedents, it is that a President in signing or withholding signature, must
consider the wisdom of the bill as one of those responsible for its character
and effect. Mr. Mason says there were only four Presidents who did not
veto bills on their merits. They were Washington, the Adamses and Jefferson. All the others have done so, and as to the four named, it is possible
that through the agency of friendly Congresses they were able to kill bills
without resorting to the veto. There are other ways of killing a cat than by
choking it with butter. It is often a good deal easier for the President to
prevent the passage of a bill by conference with friendly committees. It
does not "rock the boat" so much.

Of course vetoes are more frequent when the President and Congress
differ politically. They were very frequent in Mr. Johnson's administration
when there was bitterly opposed to him a two-thirds majority of Republicans in each House. Again in the time of Mr. Hayes, the lower House of
Congress was Democratic during his whole four years. Both Houses were
Democratic in his last two years. This led to a number of vetoes by Mr.
Hayes of bills enacted to paralyze the enforcement of Congressional election laws, and also of measures concerning the exclusion of Chinese, and
the monetary policy of the United States. In Mr. Cleveland's first term, he
had an adverse Congress, which resulted in many vetoes of special pension
bills. President Grant, President Harrison and I had to face politically hostile Congresses, which naturally led to an expressed difference of opinion
between the Executive and Congress as to the wisdom of proposed legislation. It is at such a time that one hears from the opposition Congressmen

eloquent and emphatic denunciation of "the exercise of royal prerogative by the incumbent of the White House to defeat the will of the people." When one new in the Presidential office first hears a philippic of this kind, visions of the fate of Charles I may trouble him somewhat, but after a time, especially if he has indulged the habit of reading past Congressional Records, he becomes accustomed to the well-worn expressions of legislators whom the veto of a favorite bill has disappointed. There is a well-known aphorism that men are different, but husbands are all alike. The same idea may be paraphrased with respect to Congressmen. Congressmen are different, but when in opposition to an administration they are very much alike in their attitude and in their speeches. In looking back through the Congressional debates, and in attempting to run down the history of the improvement of the White House grounds, I was much amused to read the speech of an opposition Congressman in the severest condemnation of the expenditure by President Van Buren of a comparatively small sum appropriated by Congress to improve the appearance of the grounds of the White House by some landscape gardening and tree planting. He said in effect that the President was aping the royalties of Europe in attempting to create an orangery in the rear of his palace, in which in majestic seclusion he might stretch his royal legs. As I read this speech, I could not but think that the genus of opposition Congressmen had not lost its distinctive qualities.

In the exercise of the veto power, the truth is that it often happens that the President more truly represents the entire country than does the majority vote of the two Houses. His constituency is the electorate of the United States, and by reason of that he is much freer from the influence of local prejudices and of the play of those special territorial and state interests, which, brought together by log-rolling methods, sometimes constitute a majority in both Houses for extravagant or unwise legislation. To hold up the use of the Presidential veto as an exercise of royal prerogative is of course utterly absurd. It is true that the function finds its prototype in the royal veto of the British Constitution, but no King of England has dared to exercise it for two-hundred years. He would lose his throne if he did. Under our Constitution the veto is not the act of an hereditary monarch, but of one elected by all the people to represent all the people and charged by the fundamental law with the responsibility and duty of its exercise in proper cases.

In considering a bill presented to him for signature, it is the duty of the President of course to veto a bill no matter how much he approves its expediency, if he believes that it is contrary to the constitutional limitations upon the power of Congress. He has taken an oath to the best of his ability "to preserve, protect and defend the Constitution of the United States," and he cannot escape his obligation to do so when the question before him is whether he shall approve the bill passed by both Houses which violates the Constitution he has given his plighted faith to maintain and enforce. His duty is as high and exacting in this matter as is the duty of the Supreme Court of the United States. Indeed, his function in this regard is somewhat broader than that of the Court. The question with him is whether, in his judgment, the bill is inconsistent with the Constitution. The question which the Court has to consider when an act of Congress is before it and its validity is questioned, is not whether the Court as an original question thinks the act to be a violation of the Constitution. The fact that Congress, a coordinate branch of the government, has enacted the law, and presumably has decided it to be within its legislative power, raises a very strong presumption that the act is valid. The Court, before holding otherwise, is bound to find that beyond reasonable doubt the act is not within the limit of the discretion of the legislature in construing its own powers to decide that the act in question is within those powers. When a branch of the government is vested with a power, defined and limited, it must first construe the limitations upon its own powers in exercising them; and what the Supreme Court has to say is that it has abused that discretion and beyond a reasonable doubt has transgressed its limits. It may seem that this is not a broad distinction, but practically it may be made a real one by a conscientious court. If the Court has any doubt about the validity of a law, it is bound to sustain it, and it has no right to set aside a law merely because of a difference of opinion between it and the legislature as to the legislative powers.

This difference has been emphasized by the elder Professor Thayer of Harvard in his comments on the Constitution. He has wisely and ably explained and emphasized the necessity for maintaining the distinction. A serious doubt of the validity of a proposed bill may well lead a member of

Congress to vote against it, or the President to veto it; but such a doubt would not justify the Court in treating the act as a nullity, unless it reaches an indisputable conviction that Congress has exceeded its powers, after indulging the properly strong presumption in favor of the act's validity. It may very well happen, therefore, that a President may veto a bill, Congress may pass it over his veto, the Supreme Court may sustain the law, and yet the President and the Court have the same serious doubt as to its validity which would properly lead to the President's veto but not to the Court's annulment of it after it has been passed by Congress. I can illustrate what I say by referring to a bill which I vetoed and which was passed over my veto. It was the so-called Webb bill, which declared the shipping of liquor from one state to another, where its sale was unlawful by the law of the state, to be Federally unlawful. It seemed to me that this was in effect a delegation of power to the states to make differing rules with respect to interstate commerce in something which up to this time has been regarded as a lawful subject of such commerce. If Congress wished to declare liquor an unlawful subject of commerce from one state to another, Congress would have the power; but to attribute to Congress the power to say that one state might declare something unlawful commerce among the states, while another might declare it lawful, seemed to me to be a serious interference with the proper uniform and beneficent operation of the interstate commerce clause. I properly had much less hesitation in vetoing the bill than the Supreme Court should have in declaring it to be beyond the permissible limits of Congressional discretion. In other words, the Court may entertain the same serious doubt of the validity of the bill that led to my veto of it, and still not find the question so clear as to overcome the presumption in favor of the validity of the law because Congress has enacted it. I emphasize this point because I think it is of the highest importance that the constitutional validity of a measure should be fairly considered in the legislature and by him who exercises the veto power.

English publicists have criticized the course of discussion under a written Constitution by our legislatures. They maintain that it leads to a consideration of questions of the validity of proposed legislation rather than of its expediency. I do not think that this criticism is either weighty or correct. We do not discuss the validity of the bills in the legislatures enough. The governors of the states do not consider the constitutionality of bills presented them for signature as they ought. A measure proposed is popular with the constituents of a legislator, and if a question is raised as to its constitutional validity, he is prone to say, "Well, my people wish it. If it is invalid, the court will declare it to be invalid. Therefore, why should I run the risk of incurring unpopularity when it is not my function to enforce the Constitution?" Laws are thus passed through legislatures which palpably violate the Constitution just because constituents of legislators think that the law would be a good thing. The governor signs it with the same view. The burden is thus transferred to the Court. The Court holds the law to be invalid and the popular odium arising from a defeat of the measure is visited upon the Court, which alone of the three branches of the government has respected its oath of office in the preservation of the Constitution. This is one of the fruitful sources of the unjust attacks upon the courts of the country of which we have had so many in the last ten years. You well remember the story which Mr. Roosevelt tells of a conversation which he had with the Tammany politician, Tim Campbell, when they were both members of the legislature, in which Tim appealed to him to vote for a particular bill of his and Mr. Roosevelt replied, "I cannot do it, Tim, because it is plainly unconstitutional." This called forth from Tim the well-known expression, "What the divil is the Constitution between frinds?" That is the exact spirit which has led to the neglect of their constitutional obligation by legislators, and their enactment of so many invalid measures. I have sometimes been inclined to think that after his invention and recommendation of the recall of judicial decisions, Mr. Roosevelt was leaning a little more to Tim's view of the Constitution than at the time when this conversation was held.

The Constitution provides that if the President does not return the bill presented to him within ten days (Sundays excepted) after its presentation, it is to become law just as if he had signed it, unless Congress by adjourning prevents its return, in which case it is not to become a law. This enables the President, at the close of a session, when bills are presented to him in great number, and when he usually goes to the Capitol for the purpose of signing them, just before the adjournment of Congress, to defeat a bill by what is called a pocket veto, that is by failing to sign it. If he does not return it to Congress with his objections, there is no opportunity for Congress to pass it over his veto, and therefore his failure to sign is final.

It has never been decided by the Supreme Court whether a President by signing a bill within ten days after its passage may give it validity as a law if Congress adjourns within that ten days, and before his signature. The Supreme Court has said that he may sign a bill during a recess of Congress. Practice makes it clear, however, that he may not do this after adjournment. There is only one instance of such a signature. President Monroe failed to sign a bill which he had intended to sign. After conferring with his Cabinet, he decided it was wiser to ask Congress to reënact it. President Lincoln did sign a bill after an adjournment and the bill was filed with the Secretary of State and printed among the statutes. When the matter was brought to the attention of the Senate, however, the power of the President to do so was questioned and denied, and a new bill of substantially the same purport passed both Houses and was signed by the President.

The language of the Constitution with reference to what the President shall do with a bill leaves only two alternatives, one that if he approve it, he shall sign it, the other that if he does not approve it, he shall return it with his objections to Congress. It does provide that if he fails to return it within ten days, it shall become a law, but this would seem to be only a provision for his neglect. In practice, however, some Presidents have allowed bills to become law without their signature, with the idea, I presume, that their objections to the bill do not justify a veto. Mr. Cleveland looked at the matter in this way when he allowed the Gorman-Wilson Tariff bill to become a law without his signature, though he denounced it in most emphatic terms in a letter to Mr. Catchings of the House as "an act of perfidy and dishonor." My own judgment is that the wiser course in such a case is for the President to sign the bill, with a memorandum of his reasons for doing so, in spite of his objections.

The Federal Executive veto does not include the power to veto a part of a bill. The lack of such a power in the President has enabled Congress at times to bring to bear a pressure on him to permit legislation to go through that otherwise he would veto. Appropriation bills are necessary for the life of the government, and if Congress by putting what is called a "rider" of general legislation on one of these says, "We'll hamstring the government in respect to the departments that these appropriation bills support, unless you consent to this," it puts the President in an embarrassing situation.

In President Hayes' Administration, one of the issues that he had with the Democratic Congress was in respect to the enforcement of the Federal Congressional election laws. The Democratic Congress insisted first in imposing a rider on the Military Appropriation bill for the support of the army, providing that the President should not be able to use his civil officers to maintain peace at the polls. This really had no relation to the use of the army to interfere with elections. President Hayes vetoed the bill. Congress finally passed the Army Appropriation bill without the rider, but thereupon passed the Legislative, Executive and Judicial Appropriation bill, with a similar rider, which the President again vetoed. Then Congress passed this latter appropriation bill, but in order to prevent the use of marshals to preserve peace at the polls, left out any provision for the marshals and the executive officers of the courts of the United States. That state of affairs continued for two years, to the great embarrassment of the courts. Finally, Congress surrendered after the election of President Garfield, and paid the salaries, fees and expenses of the marshals and of the executive officers of the courts which had been withheld from them for two years. In the course of the controversy, President Hayes used this language:

> The enactment of this bill into a law will establish a precedent which will tend to destroy the equal independence of the several branches of the Government. Its principle places not merely the Senate and the Executive, but the Judiciary also, under the coercive dictation of the House. The House alone will be the judge of what constitutes a grievance, and also of the means and measure of redress. An act of Congress to protect elections is now the grievance complained of; but the House may on the same principle determine that any other act of Congress, a treaty made by the President with the advice and consent of the Senate, a nomination or appointment to office, or that a decision or opinion of the Supreme Court is a grievance, and that the measure of redress is to withhold the appropriations required for the support of the offending branch of the Government.
>
> Believing that this bill is a dangerous violation of the spirit and meaning of the Constitution, I am compelled to return it to the House in

which it originated without my approval. The qualified negative with which the Constitution invests the President is a trust that involves a duty which he can not decline to perform. With a firm and conscientious purpose to do what I can to preserve unimpaired the constitutional powers and equal independence, not merely of the Executive, but of every branch of the Government, which will be imperiled by the adoption of the principle of this bill, I desire earnestly to urge upon the House of Representatives a return to the wise and wholesome usage of the early days of the Republic, which excluded from appropriation bills all irrelevant legislation.

Congress attempted the same method in my own administration, when a rider was placed upon the great Sundry Civil Appropriation bill forbidding the use of a special appropriation to enforce the anti-trust law act in prosecuting farmers and trades-unions who were found violating that act. This introduced, it seemed to me, a most pernicious discrimination and was calculated and intended to produce a lack of uniformity in the application of what should be a general law. It created a privileged class and was insisted on merely for political purposes. I vetoed the bill. A similar bill with a similar rider was subsequently signed by President Wilson, but under protest against the principle of such discrimination.

It has been suggested that such an abuse of power by Congress, for that it certainly is, could be avoided by giving to the President the power to veto special items and clauses of an appropriation bill. This power is exercised by some governors in states, notably the governor of New York. While for some purposes, it would be useful for the Executive to have the power of partial veto, if we could always be sure of its wise and conscientious exercise, I am not entirely sure that it would be a safe provision. It would greatly enlarge the influence of the President, already large enough from patronage and party loyalty and other causes. I am inclined to think that it is better to trust to the action of the people in condemning the party which becomes responsible for such riders, than to give, in such a powerful instrument like this, a temptation to its sinister use by a President eager for continued political success. This use by Congress of riders upon appropriation bills to force a President to consent to legislation which he disapproves shows a spirit of destructive factionalism and a lack of a sense of responsibility for the maintenance of the government. If such a sense of responsibility does not pervade all branches of the government, Executive, Legislative and Judicial, the government cannot remain a going concern. Instances of abuses of this sort by Congress, therefore, must be regarded as exceptional, as indeed they are, and an effort to remedy them by a change in constitutional provision would be legislation intended to pump patriotism into public officers by force. This method will certainly be found futile if such patriotism and sense of responsibility do not exist without it. If it is urged that the President should have the power to veto items in an appropriation bill to restrain Legislative extravagance, the answer is that this is not the best way. The proper remedy for that evil is the budget amendment proposed by the Constitutional Convention of New York, which I have already discussed.

2

The Minor Powers of the President

In the first chapter, I considered the general distribution of governmental powers and the veto power of the President, his only Legislative function. I now begin a consideration of his Executive functions, in some of which he or his subordinates exercise what I shall hope to show are quasi-legislative and quasi-judicial powers. In this chapter, I propose to discuss what may perhaps be called the minor functions of the President, and shall devote some of the time also to the personal aspects of the great office. I class among the President's minor functions, the powers to consult the heads of Executive departments as to the questions arising in their respective departments, to inform Congress of the state of the Union, to recommend measures to it which he may deem wise, expedient and necessary; to issue commissions to officers of the United States, and to convene Congress in extra session, and adjourn it in case of disagreement between the Houses.

The Constitution does not use the term "Cabinet," and does not recognize a Presidential Council as a legal body. There has crept into some statutes, loosely drawn, the phrase "Cabinet Officer," and the Supreme Court Judges in their discussions of cases sometimes use it. It will be observed, however, that while the Constitution refers to the head of a department and authorizes the President to make him an adviser as to matters in his own department, it contains no suggestion of a meeting of all the department heads, in consultation over general governmental matters. The Cabinet is a mere creation of the President's will. It is an extra-statutory and extra-constitutional body. It exists only by custom. If the President desired to dispense with it, he could do so. As it is, the custom is for the Cabinet to meet twice a week, and for the President to submit to its members questions upon which he thinks he needs their advice, and for the members to bring up such matters in their respective departments as they deem appropriate for Cabinet conference and general discussion.

In the British government, the Cabinet is not a statutory body. It exists there, as with us, only by custom. But this fact does not derogate from the permanence and importance of the English Cabinet, because, unlike ours, the constitution of government in Great Britain is largely by custom. The distinctive feature in the present British political structure is that a vote in the House of Commons, indicating a want of confidence in the Premier and his associates, requires their resignation; yet this only abides in custom. The English Premier in selecting his associates in his Cabinet takes those members of Parliament who will effectively cooperate with him in retaining the indispensable backing of the House of Commons majority. It is needful for a ministry, therefore, that the members of the Cabinet in such a government shall be of independent strength and influence with parliamentary members. They are partners of the Premier and not merely his appointees and advisers, and have an importance which Cabinet officers do not have with us. As a member of the government, each English Cabinet officer must be prepared on the floor of one House or the other to answer questions, defend the government, and advocate the legislation which the government urges, and for which it becomes responsible. It follows that an English Cabinet officer must have qualifications not now required of a member of a Presidential Cabinet.

I am strongly in favor of a change in our existing system, by which the importance and influence of Cabinet officers shall be increased. Without any change in the Constitution, Congress might well provide that heads of departments, members of the President's Cabinet, should be given access to the floor of each House to introduce measures, to advocate their passage, to answer questions, and to enter into the debate as if they were members, without of course the right to vote. Without any express constitutional authority, Congress has done this in the case of delegates from the territories. Why may it not therefore do it with respect to the heads of departments?

This would impose on the President greater difficulty in selecting his Cabinet, and would lead him to prefer men of legislative experience who have shown their power to take care of themselves in legislative debate. It would stimulate the head of each department by the fear of public and direct inquiry into a more thorough familiarity with the actual operations of his department and into a closer supervision of its business. On the other hand, it would give the President what he ought to have, some direct initiative in legislation and an opportunity through the presence of his competent representatives in Congress to keep each House advised of the facts in the actual operation of the government. The time lost in Congress over useless discussion of issues that might be disposed of by a single statement from the head of a department, no one can appreciate unless he has filled such a place. In my annual message, December 19, 1912, I urged this proposal upon Congress, as follows:

> This is not a new proposition. In the House of Representatives, in the Thirty-eighth Congress, the proposition was referred to a select committee of seven Members. The committee made an extensive report, and urged the adoption of the reform. The report showed that our history had not been without illustration of the necessity and the examples of the practice by pointing out that in early days Secretaries were repeatedly called to the presence of either House for consultation, advice, and information. It also referred to remarks of Mr. Justice Story in his Commentaries on the Constitution, in which he urgently presented the wisdom of such a change. This report is to be found in Volume I of the Reports of Committees of the First Session of the Thirty-eighth Congress, April 6, 1864.

Again, on February 4, 1881, a select Committee of the Senate recommended the passage of a similar bill, and made a report in which, while approving the separation of the three branches, the executive, legislative, and judicial, they point out as reason for the proposed change that, although having a separate existence, the branches are "to cooperate, each with the other, as the different members of the human body must cooperate, with each other, in order to form the figure and perform the duties of a perfect man.

The report is as follows:

> This system will require the selection of the strongest men to be heads of departments and will require them to be well equipped with the knowledge of their offices. It will also require the strongest men to be the leaders of Congress and participate in debate. It will bring these strong men in contact, perhaps into conflict, to advance the public weal, and thus stimulate their abilities and their efforts, and will thus assuredly result to the good of the country.
>
> If it should appear by actual experience that the heads of departments in fact have not time to perform the additional duty imposed on them by this bill, the force of their offices should be increased or the duties devolving on them personally should be diminished. An under-secretary should be appointed to whom could be confided that routine of administration which requires only order and accuracy. The principal officers could then confine their attention to those duties which require wise discretion and intellectual activity. Thus they would have abundance of time for their duties under this bill. Indeed, your committee believes that the public interest would be subserved if the Secretaries were relieved of the harassing cares of distributing clerkships and closely supervising the mere machinery of the departments. Your committee believes that the adoption of this bill and the effective execution of its provisions will be the first step toward a sound civil-service reform which will secure a larger wisdom in the adoption of policies and a better system in their execution.
>
> (Signed)
> Geo. H. Pendleton.
> W. B. Allison.
> D. W. Voorhees.
> J. G. Blaine.
> M. C. Butler.
> John J. Ingalls.
> O. H. Platt.
> J. T. Farley.

It would be difficult to mention the names of higher authority in the practical knowledge of our government than those which are appended to this report.

Official minutes are not kept of the Cabinet meetings. Everything is informal, except that the President sits at the head of the table, and the seats of the Cabinet members are assigned around the table according to official precedence, that is according to the order in which under the law the Cabinet officers succeed to the Presidency on the death of the President and the Vice-President, which is nearly in accordance with the order of the establishment of the various departments.

The Executive office of the President is not a recording office. The vast amount of correspondence that goes through it, signed either by the President or his Secretaries, does not become the property or a record of the government, unless it goes on to the official files of the department to which it may be addressed. The retiring President takes with him all of the correspondence, original and copies, which he carried on during his administration. Thus there is lost to public record some of the most interesting documents of governmental origin bearing on the history of an administration. It is a little like what Mr. Charles Francis Adams told me of the diplomatic records of the British Foreign Office. It has long been the custom for the important Ambassadors of Great Britain to carry on a personal correspondence with the Secretary of State for Foreign Affairs, which is not put upon the files of the department, but which gives a much more accurate and detailed account of the diplomatic relations of Great Britain than the official files. The only way in which historians can get at this, is through the good offices of the families of the deceased Ambassadors and Foreign Secretaries in whose private files they may be preserved.

Originally the State Department was supposed to be the department through which Executive acts were made public, and in which they were recorded. The Secretary of State is the custodian of the great seal of the government, and now when the President acts in general matters not affecting a particular department, and his act needs attestation by seal, the Secretary of State witnesses the signature of the President and attaches the seal. In departmental matters, however, where the President has to act, as in issuing commissions for officers in particular departments, the commissions are signed by the President, attested by the Secretary of the particular department, and a seal of that department attached. Thus the commissions of Federal Judges bear the signatures of the President and the Attorney-General, those of army officers the signatures of the President and the Secretary of War, and those of naval officers the signatures of the President and the Secretary of the Navy.

Referring again to the Cabinet meetings, Mr. Lincoln is said to have remarked that in the Cabinet after discussion and intimation of opinions, there was only one vote—and that unanimous—it was the vote of the President. It is interesting and instructive to note Mr. Jefferson's comment on the operation of the Cabinet in Washington's day. A French publicist wrote him a letter advocating a plural executive for a free government, and asked his comment upon it. He answered, dissenting from the publicist's view, and approving the plan of our Constitution as follows:

> The failure of the French Directory seems to have authorized a belief that the form of a plurality, however promising in theory, is impracticable with men constituted with the ordinary passions, while the tranquil and steady tenor of our single executive, during a course of twenty-two years of the most tempestuous times the history of the world has ever presented, gives a rational hope that this important problem is at length solved. Aided by the counsels of a Cabinet of heads of departments originally four, but now five, with whom the President consults, either singly or all together, he has the benefit of their wisdom and information, brings their views to one center, and produces a unity of action and direction in all the branches of the government. The excellence of this construction of the executive power has already manifested itself here under very opposite circumstances. During the administration of our first President, his Cabinet of four members were equally divided by as marked an opposition of principle as monarchism and republicanism could bring into conflict. Had that Cabinet been a directory, like positive and negative quantities in algebra, the opposing wills would have balanced each other and produced a state of absolute inaction. But the President heard with calmness the opinions and reasons of each, decided the course to be pursued, and kept the government steadily in it, unaffected by the agitation. The public knew well the dissensions of the Cabinet, but never had an uneasy thought on their account, because they knew also they had provided a regulating power which would keep the machine in steady movement.

The picture of the Cabinet of Washington's day, with Jefferson sitting on one side of the table and Hamilton on the other, at sword's point on most political and governmental issues, is very interesting. The admirable poise of the Father of his Country was never more clearly proven than by the fact that he was able to carry on an administration as long as he did, with such a division in his Cabinet. All Cabinets are not like this. Many of them are most harmonious, and to many of the participants such meetings bring back the pleasantest memories. Mr. Jefferson himself, in commenting on his own Cabinet, gives a very different picture from that of the Cabinet of Washington, for he says of his own Cabinet to the same correspondent, in the letter I have already referred to:

> There never arose, during the whole time, an instance of an unpleasant thought or word between the members. We sometimes met under differences of opinion, but scarcely ever failed, by conversing and reasoning, so to modify each other's ideas as to produce an unanimous result. Yet, able and amicable as the members were, I am not certain this would have been the case, had each possessed equal and independent powers. Ill-defined limits of their respective departments, jealousies, trifling at first, but nourished and strengthened by repetition of occasions, intrigues without doors of designing persons to build an importance to themselves on the divisions of others, might, from small beginnings, have produced persevering oppositions. But the power of decision in the President left no object for internal dissension, and external intrigue was stifled in embryo by the knowledge which incendiaries possessed, that no division they could foment, would change the course of the executive power.

It is noteworthy that the Cabinet in which there was more of rivalry and intrigue and bitterness than in any, except that of Washington, was Lincoln's. Thus the division of their Cabinets into cliques, the disloyalty of some of them and their conflicting ambitions greatly increased the heavy burdens of our two greatest Presidents.

The power and duty of the President to inform Congress on the state of the Union, and to recommend measures for its adoption, need very little comment, except to say that President Washington and President Adams treated the discharge of this duty as the occasion for visiting Congress in person and delivering their communications orally. The Senate in Washington's day was a small body of twenty-eight or thirty, and when the President had made a treaty, or was about to make one, and wished advice and consent of the Senate, he repaired in person to the Senate Chamber. President Washington had one annoying experience, of which Senator Maclay speaks in his diary: Through the assistance of General Knox, Secretary of War, who had dealt much with the Indians, he had made treaties with certain tribes. He went with the treaties to the Senate to ask its consent, and Knox accompanied him. Washington explained the treaties and asked their confirmation. The Senate wished to delay and put the matter over. Maclay says that he made the motion to postpone because he saw no chance of a fair investigation of a subject while the President sat there with his Secretary of War, to support his opinions and overawe the timid and neutral part of the Senate. It was suggested that the matter be referred to a committee. "As I sat down," Maclay says, "the President of the United States started up in a violent fret. 'This defeats every purpose of my coming here,' were the first words that he said. He then went on that he had brought his Secretary of War with him to give every necessary information; that the Secretary of War knew all about the business, and yet he was delayed and could not go on with the matter. However, he said he did not object to postponement until a later day." Maclay continues: "We waited for him to withdraw. He did so with a discontented air. Had he been any other man than the man whom I wish to regard as the first character in the world, I would have said, with sullen dignity. On the day appointed, the President came again, and then there was a great discussion in his presence, and a tedious discussion."

My impression is that Washington succeeded in securing the confirmation of the treaties, although Maclay does not make it clear. Another account of this, from a different source, and perhaps untrust-worthy, says that Washington was heard by one who was near to utter an oath to Knox as he left the Senate. I am not in favor of profanity and do not wish to uphold it even in so eminent a person as the Father of our Country, but I had such a similar experience in attempting to secure the advice and consent of the Senate to my General Arbitration Treaties, which another Knox presented to them, that I confess to having a warm fellow feeling for President Washington in this unlovely expression, if he uttered it. I have read much of George Washington and have always had the profoundest admiration for the qualities which he had in such a high degree, of poise, courage, serf-restraint and judgment, which without the brilliant intellectual faculties and acquirements of his contemporaries, enabled him to influence and control them all by inspiring in them a profound respect for his sense of justice, his disinterested patriotism, his high ideals, his personal force and courage and his common sense. It is difficult to get close to him as a man, however, or to feel in reading of him that personal affection that is constantly being stimulated in reminiscences of Lincoln. Such an incident as this I have related, however, of Washington shows the human side of him as a man of good red blood and makes me, because of my personal experience, come closer to him than ever before.

Jefferson had no pleasure or facility in public speaking. When he came into the office of President, therefore, he preferred to send to Congress written messages, and his practice was so formidable a precedent that this has been the custom of the Presidents down to the present administration, when President Wilson has introduced again the old practice of a personal address to both Houses. I think the change is a good one. Oral addresses fix the attention of the country on Congress more than written communications, and by fixing the attention of the country on Congress, they fix the attention of Congress on the recommendations of the President. I cannot refrain from a smile, however, when I think of the Democratic oratory which was lost because Mr. Roosevelt or I did not inaugurate such a change. The eloquent sentences that would have resounded from the lips of Senator Ollie James or Senator John Sharp Williams, those faithful followers of Jefferson, in denunciation of the introduction of "such a royal ceremony in a speech from the Throne," I could supply with little effort of the imagination. Surely a member of the Jeffersonian Party has some advantages in the Presidential chair.

It is the constitutional duty of the President to issue commissions to all officers of the United States. This, I think, is the greatest manual duty the President has to perform. When you consider all the officers in the government who are entitled to commissions, and in addition to this, the number of letters in the President's correspondence, you can understand that a substantial part of each business day is occupied with signatures. Of course the shorter the President's name, the easier his work. As I was able to sign with only seven letters, I had an advantage over my predecessor and my successor. In Washington's day, and later, all the letters patent for land and inventions had to be signed by the President, but fortunately for his more recent successors, Congress has authorized the President to designate some one else to perform this duty. I do not suppose Congress could relieve him of the burden of signing commissions, in view of the mandatory language of the Constitution.

The question of commissions seems a simple and formal one, and yet out of it came one of the greatest cases that was ever decided in this country, a case that had more direct bearing on the organic structure of this government than any in the history of the great cases decided by the Supreme Court. I refer to the case of *Marbury vs. Madison*. That case was not only of capital importance from a governmental standpoint, but it was part of the interesting personal and political history of the struggle of two giants among our statesmen and jurists. Thomas Jefferson was not in the convention that framed the Constitution. He was induced to refrain from open opposition to its ratification on a promise that a bill of rights would be added to it by amendment. In his view of government he took the democratic extreme. He was profoundly suspicious of the monarchical tendencies of the Federalist group, especially of Hamilton. As soon as the Constitution was adopted, two parties formed themselves, the Republicans and the Federalists, with Jefferson at the head of one and Hamilton at the head of the other. The Federalist Party remained in power under Washington and Adams, and then in the election of 1801, Adams was defeated by Jefferson. John Marshall, who had been a young man during the Revolution and a private soldier in the Continental Army, had taken part in the ratification of the Constitution in the Virginia Constitutional Convention, was a Federalist member of Congress in Adams' administration, and became Adams' last Secretary of State. After Adams was defeated and before Jefferson was elected and took his seat, Adams appointed Marshall to be Chief Justice, and he was confirmed in the interval by a Federalist majority in the Senate. When the Federalists saw they were going out of power, they took advantage of the fact that they controlled the Presidency and the Congress in the interval between the election and the succession of the new administration, and passed a law creating a new Circuit Court which was to be an intermediate court between the District Court and the Supreme

Court, and provision was made for the appointment of sixteen judges. President Adams appointed these judges and most of them were Federalists. They were confirmed upon the night of March 3d, preceding the 4th of March when Jefferson was to take his oath. They were known as the Midnight Judges. This action by a defeated party roused the indignation of Jefferson and the Republicans. Madison, whom Jefferson designated to act as Secretary of State, was very prompt and insistent, so tradition has it, in taking over from Marshall, who continued to act as Secretary till the close of Adams' term, the Department of State. It is said that Marshall in commenting on Madison's urgency felicitated himself that he got away from the office with his own hat. The Republican Party was determined to abolish the Midnight Judges, and they promptly passed a law for this purpose. When the law was on its passage, it was argued by the Federalists that it was unconstitutional because United States Judges must hold their offices for life. Fearing that John Marshall, who had then taken his seat as Chief Justice, and his Federalist colleagues in the Supreme Court might reach this conclusion, Congress postponed the time for the meeting of the Court for more than a year. When the Court met, no effort was made to test the validity of the repeal of the Circuit Court Act, but a cause was presented involving an issue quite as personal to Jefferson and Madison. Adams had appointed one Marbury to be Justice of the Peace in the District of Columbia for five years. The Senate confirmed him. Adams signed the Commission and sent it to Marshall as Secretary of State, who signed it and attached the seal. By some oversight, it was not delivered to the appointee, and Adams and Marshall went out of office. Marbury thereupon applied to Madison for it, and Madison declined to deliver it. Marbury filed a petition in the Supreme Court of the United States for a mandamus to compel Madison to deliver him the Commission. An Act of Congress authorized a proceeding in mandamus in the Supreme Court, but the restrictions upon the jurisdiction of the Court in the Constitution forbade it. For the first time there was flatly presented the question whether the Supreme Court was bound to take an act of Congress duly passed by that body as conclusively valid, or, if the Court found the act to be in violation of the Constitution, it could hold the law invalid and proceed as if the law had never been passed. This was the great issue in the case, and it is this which constitutes its transcendent importance.

The Chief Justice, speaking for the Court, held that in any case coming before it in which the rights of the parties were affected by what purported to be a statute of Congress, the Court could not avoid deciding whether it was the law or not; that when there was an inevitable inconsistency between the statutory law and the fundamental law, the statutory law must yield to fundamental law and be held void.

The Chief Justice in his opinion sustained this conclusion not only on general principles controlling the action of a court under a written Constitution limiting legislative powers, but he enforced it by reference to the express language of the Constitution itself in respect to the Court's jurisdiction and the supremacy of the Constitution. This decision thus made the Judicial branch of the government the branch which could effectively determine the limits of power of the other two branches. It became a precedent for similar action by courts in all the states, and for more than one hundred years it has been accepted as authoritative. Jefferson denounced it as usurpation of Judicial power. Every once in a while we have a recurrence of this criticism. Such an attack figured very prominently in the general onslaught on courts that was made by the Progressive Party in agitating recall of judges and recall of judicial decisions.

The conclusion as to the invalidity of the law under which the petition for mandamus in *Marbury vs. Madison* was filed disposed of the case. The Chief Justice, however, was not content to allow the case to go off in this way. Before deciding the question of jurisdiction, he seized the opportunity to pass upon the merits of the issue by deciding that if the Court had jurisdiction, it must issue the writ and compel Mr. Madison to deliver the Commission. He said that this was a duty of the Secretary which did not involve any discretion after the appointment had been made and the Commission had been signed and sent him for delivery. Such an expression of opinion was what the lawyers call *obiter dictum*. It was not necessary to the decision of the case before the Court. It was prompted by the political feelings of the Chief Justice and his colleagues and a willingness to criticize Madison and Jefferson. Here was the beginning of that long duel between Marshall and Jefferson. Marshall stood for the broad, liberal Federalistic construction of the Constitution, treating it as the expression of the whole people of the United States in founding a nation, while Jefferson insisted that it was nothing but a league of the independent states granting limited and delegated powers to a weak central government. Jefferson's term of office continued for eight years. He was followed by Madison and then by Monroe, over both of whom he seems to have exercised influence. Meantime Marshall continued on the Supreme Bench and lived ten years after Jefferson. Jefferson was the father, and until he died in 1825, the real head, of a great party which, with but a few short intervals, continued in power until the Civil War. Yet Marshall, a Federalist, in his service of more than a third of a century at the head of the Court, was able to breathe into the Constitution the spirit of nationality and of Federal supremacy so effectively that a court of Democrats succeeding him did not destroy his work. Marshall's construction of the Constitution is the fundamental law today, acquiesced in by all.

Both Marshall and Jefferson were great men. Marshall was probably the greatest judge that ever lived, when one considers the wonderful cogency and beauty of his judicial style, his statesman's foresight, the accuracy of his legal learning, the power of his reasoning, his soundness of judgment, his wonderful personal influence over his colleagues and the fateful influence of his work upon the structure of our great government. Jefferson had profound confidence in the people, and was the embodiment of the democratic principle. He was a genius in many ways. He was a voluminous and enormously industrious correspondent. He was a student of government and a statesman, a lawyer, an architect, a politician, a man of widest interests and information, the champion of all freedom and especially of religious tolerance, the founder of the University of Virginia, and a great promoter of education in that early day.

Though unnecessary to the decision, the principle of law laid down by Marshall in *Marbury vs. Madison* as to the right of a court to command the head of a department to do a ministerial duty, involving the exercise of no discretion, has been followed by the Supreme Court in several cases. In one case Congress directed that the Postmaster General credit certain contractors with the government with amounts to be ascertained by accounting officers. The Postmaster General refused to do this, and the Supreme Court held that a mandamus would lie to compel him to do it. In another case, the case of *Decatur vs. Paulding,* Congress had provided a pension for men and officers in the navy, to be granted by the Secretary of the Navy. Decatur's widow claimed that she was entitled to the pension under the law, and asked the Court to rule that she was thus entitled and to direct the Secretary of the Navy to allow her the pension. The Court held that in this case under the law Congress intended to entrust the granting of the pension to the official judgment of the Secretary of the Navy and that the Court would not control such Executive discretion. The distinction is to be found in the purpose of Congress. If that which remains to be done by the Executive officer does not involve and was not intended by Congress to involve discretion in doing it on the part of the Executive, then the courts can compel the Executive to do the act, but if any discretion is entrusted to the Executive, then the court is powerless. In the reconstruction period, after the Civil War, when Congress passed an act enabling the President to institute a military government in each of the conquered seceding states, suits were brought to enjoin the President from carrying out the law, on the ground that the law was invalid. The Court refused to enjoin the President, on the ground that even if the law was unconstitutional, the function of the President under the law was a political one with which the Court could not interfere, and this view was further enforced by the admitted impotency of the Court to restrain the President from carrying out the law if he believed it to be constitutional. This field of Judicial control over Executive action and the line between it and that in which there is no such control, offers an opportunity for the study of nice distinctions which I shall not, for lack of space, further pursue.

The President has power to convene Congress in extraordinary session, and to adjourn Congress when the Houses disagree as to adjournment, to such time as he may think proper.

When I convened Congress in extraordinary session to pass the Reciprocity bill, the leaders of the Democratic majority in the House were fearful that the Senate might attempt to adjourn after the bill was passed, and that the House might not have the opportunity of enacting some tariff bills for political use in the next election. The Democratic leaders therefore came to me to know whether I intended to exercise the power of adjourning the House in case of a disagreement. It had been reported that that was my plan. I had never thought of it and was able to assure them of this.

In a recent controversy between the Houses as to adjournment, an appeal was made to President Wilson to adjourn them. This power of prorogation, I was inclined to think when I was in the White House, was limited to the adjournment of an extra session of Congress, but I did not give the question full consideration. As I read it now, I think that the power of adjournment where the Houses differ over the question of adjournment can be exercised by the President at any session of Congress. No President has ever attempted to use this power.

The constitutional functions of the President seem very broad, and they are. When many speak of his great power, they have in mind that what the President does, goes, like kissing, by favor. I beg of you to believe that the Presidency offers but few opportunities for showing power of this sort. The responsibility of the office is so heavy, the earnest desire that every man who fills the place has to deserve the approval of his countrymen by doing the thing that is best for the country is so strong, and the fear of just popular criticism is so controlling, that it is difficult for one who has borne the burden of the office for four years to remember more than a few favors that he was able to confer. There are certain political obligations that the custom of a party requires the President to discharge on the recommendation of Senators and Congressmen. I hope to point out in the next chapter how that kind of obligation should be reduced to a minimum by a change of law. I refer now, however, to a different kind of power with which popular imagination clothes the President, that of gratifying one man, humiliating another, or punishing a third, in order to satisfy the pleasure, the whim or vengeance of a ruler. That does not exist. The truth is that great as his powers are, when a President comes to exercise them, he is much more concerned with the limitations upon them than he is affected, like little Jack Horner, by a personal joy over the big personal things he can do.

The President is given the White House to live in,—a very comfortable, homelike house. In all the world, I venture to say, there is no more appropriate official residence for a chief executive, or one better adapted to the simple democratic taste of the American people, than the White House. It is dignified, it is beautiful, it is commodious. It offers an opportunity for proper entertainment of the President's guests. It is much less extensive and much less ornate than the royal palaces of Europe, yet it is quite ample to surround the occupant with that dignified freedom from intrusion which the President ought to have.

There is an impression that the President cannot leave the country and that the law forbids. This is not true. The only law which bears on the subject at all is the constitutional provision that the Vice-President shall take his place when the President is disabled from performing his duties. Now if he is out of the country at a point where he cannot discharge the necessary functions that are imposed upon him, such disability may arise, but the communication by telegraph, wireless and by telephone are now so good that it would be difficult for a President to go anywhere out of the country and not be able to keep his subordinates in constant information as to his whereabouts and his wishes. As a custom, Presidents do not leave the country. Occasionally it seems in the public interest that he should. President Roosevelt visited the Canal Zone for the purpose of seeing what work was being done there and giving zest to it by personal contact with those who were engaged in it. I did the same thing later on, traveling, as he did, on the deck of a government vessel, which is technically the soil of the United States, from Hampton Roads to the Canal Zone under the dominion of the United States. We were not out of the jurisdiction except for a few hours. He went into the City of Panama, as I did, and dined with the President of the Panamanian Republic. So, too, I dined with President Diaz at Juarez in Mexico, just across the border from El Paso. Nobody was heard to say that in any of these visits we had disabled ourselves from performing our constitutional and statutory functions.

The assassination of three Presidents led Congress to provide that the Chief of the Secret Service should furnish protection to the President as he moves about either in Washington or in the country at large. While President, I never was conscious of any personal anxiety in large crowds, and I have been in many of them. Yet the record is such that Congress would be quite derelict if it disregarded it. These guards are a great burden to the President. He never can go anywhere that he does not have to inflict upon those whom he wishes to visit the burden of their presence. It is a little difficult for him to avoid the feeling after a while that he is under surveillance rather than under protection. The Secret Service men are level-headed, experienced and of good manners, and they are wise in their methods. If a person is determined to kill a President and is willing to give up his life to do it, no such protection will save him. But desperate persons of this kind are very rare. The worst danger is from those who have lost part

45

or all of their reason and whom the presence of the President in the immediate neighborhood excites. I may be mistaken, but it seems to me that with such experts as we now have, the assassination of President McKinley in Buffalo might possibly have been avoided. Under the practice that the secret service men now pursue in a public reception, a man with a hand in his pocket would not be permitted to approach within striking or shooting distance of the President. His holding a revolver under his handkerchief in his pocket would now be detected long before he could get within reach of the object of his perverted purpose. He would find the hand of the Secret Service man thrust into the pocket to find what his own was doing there. Had this been done in the case of the assassin at Buffalo, that tragedy would probably not have occurred.

The President so fully represents his party, which secures political power by its promises to the people, and the whole government is so identified in the minds of the people with his personality that they are inclined to make him responsible for all the sins of omission and of commission of society at large. This would be ludicrous if it did not have sometimes serious results. The President cannot make clouds to rain and cannot make the corn to grow, he cannot make business good; although when these things occur, political parties do claim some credit for the good things that have happened in this way. He has no power over state legislation, which covers a very wide field and which comes in many respects much closer to the happiness of the people than the Federal government.

Some urge, because the states have not shown themselves as active as they ought to be in suppressing evils and accomplishing good, that the United States government should thereby acquire additional authority, and the President and Congress should assume new functions. This would break up our whole Federal System. The importance of that system is frequently misunderstood. Its essence is in the giving through the states local control to the people over local affairs and confining national and general subjects to the direction of the central government. Our experience with the administration of the public lands, with the control of our national mineral wealth, with the irrigation system of arid lands which we have undertaken, and with the disposition of the many sources of water power owned by the United States, all show that it is exceedingly difficult for the central government to administer what in their nature are local matters and put in force a uniform national policy as to these subjects that may often be at variance with the local view. A centralized system of government, in which the President and Congress regulated the doorsteps of the people of this country, would break up the Union in a short time. Those who lightly call for this extension really do not understand the dangerous proposition they are urging.

While the President's powers are broad, the lines of his jurisdiction are as fixed as a written constitution can properly make them. He has tremendous responsibilities. Every President does the best he can, and while we may differ with him in judgment, while we may think he does not bring the greatest foresight to his task, while we may think that he selects poor instruments for his assistants and therefore we may properly vote against his reëlection to the office, we must remember that while he is in office, he is the head of our government. We should indulge in his favor the presumption that he acts under a high sense of duty. Correct ideals and disciplined intelligence should impose a special responsibility on men and women as law-abiding American citizens to be respectful to constituted authority and to the President, because it was the American people who chose him, and for the time being he is the personal embodiment and representative of their dignity and majesty.

3

The Power of Appointment

One of the functions which in a practical way gives the President more personal influence than any other is that of appointments. The prestige that a President has in the outset of his administration is in part due to this power. Even in the case of the most popular President, his prestige wanes with Congress as the term wears on and the offices are distributed. Mr. Evarts, in referring to filling consular places, said, "Some we appointed and more we disappointed." " 'Tis true, 'tis pity, and pity 'tis, 'tis true."

Under the Constitution, Ambassadors, Public Ministers, Consuls, Judges of the Supreme Court and other officers of the United States, whose appointment is not otherwise provided for, are to be appointed by the President, with the advice and consent of the Senate. Congress is permitted to vest the appointment of inferior officers in the President alone, in the courts of law or in the heads of departments. Heads of departments could hardly be called inferior officers—at least they would object to such an interpretation—though Senators and Congressmen sometimes call them so. The language of the Constitution thus leaves it doubtful whether Congress could give the selection of his Cabinet to the President without confirmation by the Senate. The question will not trouble us, however, for the Senate is never likely to consent to waive the right it now has, to pass upon the President's choice of his official family.

As a matter of fact, all the important offices, and a great many offices that are not important, in addition to the ones especially mentioned in the Constitution, are filled by the President, by and with the advice and consent of the Senate. The President alone is authorized by Congress to appoint comparatively few officers. There are minor officers in great number, notably the fourth-class postmasters, that are appointed by the head of a department. The Clerks of the courts and the United States Commissioners are appointed by the judges of the respective courts.

It was settled, as long ago as the first Congress, at the instance of Madison, then in the Senate, and by the deciding vote of John Adams, then Vice-President, that even where the advice and consent of the Senate was necessary to the appointment of an officer, the President had the absolute power to remove him without consulting the Senate. This was on the principle that the power of removal was incident to the Executive power and must be untrammeled. In the administration of Andrew Johnson, the Republican Congress regarded the President as an apostate and a traitor to Republican principles. With a two-thirds majority in each House, it sought to reverse this principle as to the power of removal by the tenure of office act. Its first section continued a person in an office in which he had been confirmed by the Senate, until the appointment and qualification of his successor. This of course made his removal dependent upon the advice and consent of the Senate to the appointment of a successor, and put the question of removal, therefore, completely within the control of the Senate. The act further especially provided that the head of a department should hold his office during the term of the President who appointed him, and should be subject to removal only by consent of the Senate. This grew out of Mr. Johnson's removal of Mr. Stanton from the War Office. When President Grant came into office, much of the act was repealed at his instance. It never came before the courts directly in such a way as to invite a decision on its validity, but there are intimations in the opinions of the Supreme Court that in the tenure of office act Congress exceeded its legislative discretion.

As we look back upon the history of Johnson's administration, and can remember the extreme and passionate feeling entertained by good, moral, patriotic men toward Mr. Johnson, and the measures to which they were willing to resort in order to deprive him of his official power, and indeed of his office, we have a most significant illustration of the wisdom of limitations in a written Constitution, imposed by a highly intelligent people in their calm and deliberative moments upon action which may be taken by themselves under the influence of passion and prejudice. Now that the period has become history, and a half century passed, we realize that it would have been a blot upon the fairness of the American people to have removed Mr. Johnson, with all his temperamental defects, on the grounds charged in the impeachment articles, and we rejoice that there were dissentient Republicans enough to prevent the majority of votes in favor of the impeachment from reaching the necessary two-thirds. It was a great deal better to put up with the gross mistakes involved in Mr. Johnson's policies from a Republican point of view, than it was by a strained and unfair construction of the Constitution and of the evidence advanced, to remove him from his office on the ground that he had committed high crimes and misdemeanors in its administration. It is useful to dwell on this one of many notable instances in the history of every popular government, to refute the proposition upon which the recall of judges, the recall of judicial decisions, the attack upon written Constitutions and upon the system of their judicial interpretation and enforcement is based. That proposition is that because the people have and ought to have the power to adopt the written Constitution and to amend it, therefore they are fitted to interpret and apply the Constitution, and in effect amend it, in a particular case between particular individuals. This is an egregious fallacy. The best and most intelligent men, well able wisely to frame and adopt a written Constitution laying down general limitations, in accordance with general principle, nevertheless may, and often do, lose their fairness and clearness of vision over a special case between special individuals arousing personal or party passion.

According to the last report of the United States Civil Service Commission, the number of officers and employees in the executive civil service, on the 30th of June, 1913, was 469,879. With the increase in the offices which occurred in the last Congress, and with the actual increase that follows the growth of the population, it will soon be half a million. By the activities of these civil servants, the Federal government maintains its personal presence, so to speak, in every local community throughout the vast stretch of national jurisdiction. In the days before the present civil service law, a sense of obligation to the President for the places held, made practically all the civil employees his political henchmen. In those halcyon times, even the humblest charwoman or the most poorly paid janitor felt a throb of deep personal interest in the political health of the President.

Machine politics and the spoils system are as much an enemy of a proper and efficient government system of civil service as the boll weevil is of the cotton crop, or the various forms of insects and blight are of the farmer and the horticulturist in their pursuits. The strength of these pernicious influences has not been entirely destroyed by the present Federal civil service law. I think, however, their evil has been more mitigated in the Federal civil service system than in the states where there is a merit system. In the rush of reform in the last decade, I believe nine of the states have adopted the competitive civil service system and a requirement for its adoption has been incorporated in the charters of 250 cities. The Federal system, is older and much better enforced. The difficulty, however, that we encounter is the same as in the carrying out of many reforms. The securing of the necessary legislation proves to be only a necessary initial step, but perhaps not the most important and difficult one. The law will not enforce itself. It has accomplished one purpose in enabling those who voted for it in the legislature to claim credit for it on the stump. But such a law cannot be drawn, which will be practical, and at the same time will not permit evasion of its purpose by a politician in the executive chair who devotes his time to it. We often therefore find the law more honored in the breach than in the observance. The life of a civil service system on the merit principle is in its executive enforcement, and that only comes with a gradual improvement in the public scrutiny and the official conscience in respect to the law. If a party remains in power for a number of successive terms, the merit system acquires a stronger hold than where frequent changes from one party to another in the executive administration tempt the seizure of patronage for party purposes by hook or crook. Still we should not be disheartened. Defective as the Federal system law has proved to be in certain ways, the principle has made great headway since it was adopted in 1883. The positions then affected by it numbered about 14,000. On June 30th,

1913, the positions affected were more than 282,000, and of these 172,000 were brought under the law by executive orders extending the system, while 110,000 were included by the natural expansion of the service after the orders had become effective. About 190,000 positions under the government are not subject to competitive examination. Of these 10,000 are Presidential appointees. The remainder are laborers or contracting employees whose exclusion from the classified service is doubtless justified by the conditions. It is with respect to the 10,000 Presidential employees that a real improvement can be brought about. They are most of them local Federal officers distributed throughout the United States, first, second and third class postmasters, collectors of customs, collectors of internal revenue and public land officers. They must be confirmed by the Senate. Where an appointment is subject to confirmation by the Senate, it cannot by executive order be put in the classified civil service. Congress might, however, repeal the necessity for confirmation and give the appointments to the President alone. He then could classify them all and incorporate them in the merit system, and the appointments to such places would be filled by promotions from subordinate positions of assistants. Thus all the local offices throughout the country, the postmasters, the collectors of internal revenue, the collectors of customs, and all other subordinates, would be given permanent tenure and appointed and promoted after examination and upon proved efficiency. The retention by Congress of the necessity for confirmation by the Senate enables members to keep these local offices out of the classified service, and to make them the football of politics. In effect, it enables them to administer these offices as personal patronage, under a custom which is established through the so-called courtesy of the Senate. Under it, the partisan majority in the Senate will usually decline to confirm an appointment made by the President to a postmastership or a collectorship, which is not recommended by the Senators or Congressmen from the district in which the appointee lives and is to discharge his duties. There is a clear understanding between Senators and Congressmen as to how this patronage is to be divided between them in each state, and the President attempting to break up the custom has heretofore found himself unable to do so.

There have been notable instances, as in the case of President Garfield and Senators Conkling and Platt, where the President asserted his right to act without the recommendation of the New York Senators in a New York appointment. Public sympathy ran with the President in this controversy, as it generally does, but tradition and the advantage of cohesion in the Senate make it difficult to overcome the custom. More than this, in the Garfield-Conkling controversy, it was not a question of civil service reform. The issue was political. It was only a question whether a Conkling man should be replaced by a Blaine man, and it was a question whether Mr. Garfield should be permitted to pay a political debt of Mr. Blaine by the appointment of Mr. Blaine's friend, Judge Robertson, and the removal of a friend of Senator Conkling. Nor did Mr. Garfield seek to change the custom except in this case. In one of his state papers he expressly advocated the system of recommendations for such appointments by Congressmen and Senators. From time to time in the present administration, there have been threatened issues over confirmations between the President and the Senate, growing out of party factional differences, but they have been smoothed over, and I think it will be found generally that the Senate has maintained the custom of which I have spoken. An attempt on the President's part to break up the custom would create a factional opposition which would interfere with the passing of the bills he recommends, and endanger the successful carrying out of the policies to which he is pledged.

Any discussion of the subject is lacking which does not make some reference to the solemn argument of solemn Senators in the effort to enlarge the meaning of the words "advice and consent of the Senate," used by the Constitution in describing the part the Senate should play in the matter of appointments. The usual contention is that these words require that the President, before making a nomination, consult the Senate. To use Skipper Jack Bunsby's language, as reported in *Dombey and Son,* "The bearings of this observation is in the application on it." Such a construction of the term "advice and consent" easily leads one imbued with the sacred awfulness of the Senate's function in the government to the conclusion that a Republican President under the Constitution and the courtesy of the Senate must consult the Republican Senators from a state before making an appointment in that state, although no such constitutional or statutory obligation is upon him in respect of Democratic Senators. The Constitution thus varies in its application to the power of Senators of one political party and to the Senators of another. This is not entirely humorous, much as it may seem to be. A Senator asked me to appoint two men, one to be District Attorney, and the other his assistant, and requested that they be allowed to divide the aggregate salary of the two offices equally. When I declined to do so, he requested the appointment of one of them to the chief office. Upon investigation, I did not think his standing at the bar was such as to justify the appointment, and was confirmed in this opinion by his willingness to accept the office under the arrangement as suggested. I nominated another lawyer of much higher capacity and greater fitness, who was also a political supporter of the Senator. He fought the nomination on the ground that with devilish ingenuity I had sought to embarrass him. While he admitted the competency and high character of my nominee and his proper political views, he argued that as his advice to me had been different, and as he in such local matters represented the Senate, and had not advised and consented to the nomination, the appointment should not be confirmed, in his view of the constitutional function of the Senate in appointments. I should, in fairness, say that the Senate did not sanction his view.

As long as these important local offices remain political, and are the patronage of Senators and Congressmen, the expense of the administration of the offices will be largely more than it need be. I was much interested during my term of office in devising a system for the permanent promotion of efficiency and economy in the government service. I induced Congress to give me $100,000 a year for two years, to pay the expenses of an expert Commission, to examine the governmental business and make reports upon the changes needed by the introduction of modern business methods and economy, to enable the people to get more for their money. The reports that they made, by which they pointed out needed changes in our present system, including the budget, which I described in my first chapter, were not popular with Congress, especially not with the last Congress of my term. The necessary appropriation was withdrawn. The Commission, however, did a great deal of most useful work, and while the dust is accumulating on their reports at present, their investigations and conclusions were of permanent value, and some day they will be made the basis for further investigation and for definite measures of reform. Among other conclusions which they reached, and which makes a reference to their work relevant here, was that the requirement for confirmation by the Senate of these local Federal offices, numbering about 10,000, should be repealed, and that the force in all the offices should be reclassified, and all, including the chief officers, should be put in the classified service. They reported that if this was done, the chief offices might be abolished and the work be done by the present assistants, whose salaries could be increased 20 percent. In this way the work of the government would be more effectively done by the assistants who are usually experts, and there would be a saving of $4,500,000 a year.

Not only would the government's business be better done, but there would be eliminated opportunity for the use of Federal appointments to influence or control political nominations and elections, an abuse which has greatly helped the maintenance of machine politics and the success of professional political positions. I recommended such a change in my four annual messages, but Congress took no notice of the suggestion. Congressmen and Senators have an impression that to lose this patronage would very seriously interfere with their political future and power. I do not mean to say that some Congressmen and some Senators do not make such patronage politically useful for themselves, but I venture to think, and the judgment of men of much greater political experience and observation than I have had will sustain me, that the having, and use of, such patronage more often injures than helps the user in securing his renomination and reëlection. It is a saying in Washington, justified by the fact, that an appointment of a first, second, third or fourth class postmaster not infrequently creates for the Congressman who secures it one ingrate and ten enemies.

Candor compels me to refer to some dangers in our extension of the classified service and permanent tenure of employees. Substantial progress toward better things can rarely be taken without developing new evils requiring new remedies. In the classified system, there are large bodies of mail carriers, postal mail clerks, and of other subordinate civil servants, who have a common interest in an increase in their salary or other terms of their employment. They form associations or in effect trades-unions. They perfect their organizations. They publish a newspaper. Their government duties carry them into close contact with the people and voters of the various Congressional districts, and in indirect ways they seek to bring undue political pressure upon the members of Congress and the Senate to accomplish their personal desires. They are often successful in this. It is a pernicious use of the opportunities given by their official duties to secure an advance of their pay or other more favorable terms of service, on other grounds than the merit of the question. Executive orders have been issued to prevent such activities, but the demagogues of both Houses and both parties rush forward to hamper Executive authority in this respect, and the evil thus far has continued. It has been used as an argument against the classified competitive system. It seems to me the proper view to take of this is that we must find some means to prevent such an abuse, but that it should not be a reason for losing the great advantage of the merit system.

I cannot exaggerate the waste of the President's time and the consumption of his nervous vitality involved in listening to Congressmen's intercession as to local appointments. Why should the President have his time taken up in a discussion over the question who shall be postmistress at the town of Devil's Lake in North Dakota? How should he be able to know, with confidence, who is best fitted to fill such a place? If we were to follow ordinary business methods in a matter which concerns business only and does not concern general political policies, as we ought to do, would we not leave such appointments to the natural system of promotion for efficiency? If the persons and parties contending for the abolition of bosses and the suppression of machines would show the faith and sincerity that ought to be in them, they could promote the cause which they so loudly proclaim, most effectively, by passing the law which I recommended to Congress. Votes upon such a measure would be a test of their sincerity in this matter. I regret to say that up to this time, few members of any party, whether Republican, Democratic or Progressive, however drastic reformers, have stood this test. Of course there were machines that were corrupt and there were bosses that made a profession of politics and held themselves out as political attorneys to be retained. There are not so many now. A great reform in this respect has been effected. But parties are essential to the success of popular government, and parties mean organization. It is not without humor to note the effect upon the enthusiastic purist and reformer in politics when a consciousness of this steals over him, and he begins to look with tenderness upon the use of patronage to help the organization of the party which was founded in the interest of pure reform.

We find that often the difference between political machines and a party organization for reform is only determined by the question, "Is it for you or against you?" If it is for you and your ideas, it is a justifiable organization, and the more effective you can make it, the better. If it is against you, it is a low political machine and ought to be condemned out of the mouths of all decent people. If the leader of the organization is with you, he is a political leader with a statesmanlike view. If he is against you, he is a boss, and the typical head of a dangerous machine. This personal element and this distinction between the evil use of patronage and the good use of patronage are the two obstructions to a betterment of our civil service system. Everything that tends to arbitrary and complete power in any officer in the distribution of offices, whose duties do not affect the determination of political policies, is demoralizing. It gives sanction to favoritism, and favoritism develops abuses even where its exercise is entrusted to the best men.

The law puts the appointment of clerks of courts in the judges. Judges are men of high character, great ability and wide learning generally, but when they are given executive or quasi-political functions, that is, when they exercise patronage, they have proven to be quite like other men. Clerks appointed in the Federal district courts become part of the family of the judge. Their appointments are practically for life. They feel secure. They are close to the judge. Their associations are intimate. They naturally seek to increase the earnings of their offices, especially when their salaries are more or less dependent on the amount of their official earnings, and they are prone to overcharges. The favor they enjoy with the judge as part of his family has, I am sorry to say, permitted such abuses. The reluctance that some judges have to call their clerks to strict account in the management of their offices is too well known to the head of the Department of Justice, and to his inspectors, whose duty it is to examine their accounts. When in office, I recommended that the President have the power of removal of such clerks for cause, upon the report of the Attorney-General, but no such action was taken, although there were a number of cases presented justifying such a change in the law. With nearly one hundred clerks of courts, and with a larger number of deputies spread all over the United States, the influence that can be used with members of Congress in a matter like this, not acutely political, only those who have had occasion to meet it can fully understand.

In order to protect the judges against their unjudicial selves in extra judicial matters, I would remove all patronage from the courts. The patronage of the Lord Chancellor in England is very large indeed, and it does not tend to the higher standing of that great judicial officer. Lord Westbury, one of the ablest Chancellors England ever had, was compelled to resign because of a difficulty growing out of the patronage which he had exercised in behalf of a member of his family who had abused his office. I would vest the appointment of receivers in equity to take charge of railroads by the Federal courts in the Interstate Commerce Commission. They could be made of course quite as subject to the direction of the court, though appointed by another authority, as if appointed by the court itself. I know whereof I speak as to the wisdom of such a change. For eight years I acted as a circuit judge, and during much of that time, I was engaged through receivers in operating many thousands of railroads within my circuit. The executive power of appointment the court is thus called upon to exercise is not good for the court, creates antagonisms that ought to be avoided, and interferes with the proper discharge of normal judicial functions. The vesting in courts of the appointment of supervisors of election under the Federal election laws before their repeal was greatly detrimental to the standing of the Federal courts and necessarily had the effect to drag them into partisan controversy. In the South, because the judges were generally of the opposite political complexion from that of the great body of the voters, it made the courts for the time being alien courts. Since the abolition of the Federal election laws and the appointments of a number of Democratic judges in the South, I think the standing of the Federal courts with the people of that section has become changed for the better.

In my judgment, the President should not be required to exercise his judgment to make appointments except to fill the most important offices. In the Executive department, he should be limited to the selection of those officers, the discharge of whose duties involves discretion in the carrying out of the political and governmental policy of his administration. He therefore ought to have the appointment of his Cabinet officers, and he ought also to have the appointment of a political under-secretary in each department to take the place of the head of the department when for any reason the head of the department is not able to discharge his usual duties. All other officers in the departments, including the Assistant Secretaries and the Chiefs of Bureaus, should have a permanent tenure and not change with each administration. This would greatly facilitate the continuity of the government and prevent the halt and lack of efficiency that necessarily attend a change in the Assistant Secretaries in each department and in the Chiefs of all Bureaus. For a year or a year and a half, at least, sometimes for a longer period, it throws the administration of the department into the complete control of minor subordinates, the Chiefs of Divisions and Chief Clerks, and makes the inexperienced heads of departments, Assistant Secretaries and Chiefs of Bureaus entirely dependent on such subordinates.

Consider the entirely unnecessary helplessness of our government in the administration of our foreign relations, in which there is a greater necessity for continuity of policy than in any other department, when men having no practical knowledge of the previous foreign policy of the government, its safe traditions or of diplomatic custom, are substituted for competent officials. When such changes are possible, we put ourselves at a great disadvantage in dealing with the departments of foreign affairs of other countries, and this disadvantage is accentuated and increased when competent representatives abroad in our diplomatic service are removed and men of no experience replace them. The President of course should appoint the Supreme Judges, as the Constitution requires, and the inferior judges of the Federal judiciary. He ought, too, to appoint the general officers of the army and the flag officers of the navy, and he ought also to appoint the leading Ambassadors and Ministers. Other appointments, it seems to me, might well be left to a system of promotion, to be carried on under civil service rules as interpreted and enforced by a Commission and the heads of departments. In this way, the attention of the President would be taken up in matters of appointment with those offices in which he would have a full opportunity to learn of the qualifications of proper candidates, and in the appointment of which, because of the conspicuous importance of the duties to be discharged, he would be held to a proper responsibility by a much more discriminating public scrutiny than can possibly be exercised in respect to the less important and subordinate offices.

I have spoken of the drain upon the nervous vitality of the President in the consideration of the many subordinate offices that he has to fill and the constant interviews that he is bound to have with Congressmen and

with Senators over such appointments, and the disputes and friction incident to the decision in such cases. One cannot go through the strain of the
Presidential office, especially in such cases, unless he has a sense of humor.
That takes up the jolts, and it lightens the monotonous and annoying routine and gives an opportunity for a study of the play of motives in human
nature. No one has as good opportunity to know Senators and Congressmen as the President, because in asking the Presidential favor, the Senator
or Congressman frequently bares his motives and discloses his inmost traits
of character in the confidence and secrecy of the Executive office. It is more
or less an unconscious confessional. It enables the President to measure the
characters of men in public life. He finds that some popular idols have feet
of clay, and that others not held in great public esteem have sturdier virtues
and more disinterested anxiety for the public weal than their press-made
reputations would indicate.

Sometimes the incidents are farcical and mirthmaking. I remember
one case of the wife of a politician of influence, who was anxious to secure
an appointment for her son. She procured the recommendation of Congressmen and Senators in both parties, and to see that they said what she
wished them to say, she accompanied them to the Executive office. When
the appointment, which was for a technical place, was given to another, she
wrote me a letter, most severe, in which she arraigned me for ingratitude in
not giving her permanent happiness, as I might, by the turn of my hand,
when she had secured a number of votes for a bill in the passage of which
I was much interested as an administration measure. I wrote to her in as
gentle a way as possible to break the blow to a mother's heart and supposed
that the incident was closed; but an accidental delay in the confirmation
led to the writing of a letter in the name of her husband, but in her hand-
writing, in which I was advised that she was seriously ill in bed with a
disease usually fatal and which was injuriously affected by the mental worry
which I had given her by a failure to make the appointment which she
sought. The letter requested that I withdraw the name which had been
sent in and appoint her son in order that she might rise again from what
otherwise would be her last illness. I wrote another sympathetic letter explaining why this could not be done. The appointment I had made was
confirmed immediately after, and within two days this lady and her husband were the first guests to greet Mrs. Taft and me at a White House

musicale, without the slightest evidence of any illness at all, and with an attractive smile which seemed to say, "That episode is ended and we are on good terms still."

A lady of charming appearance and manner, elegantly gowned, came to me when I was Secretary of War, and asked that her son be admitted to West Point. The son had been appointed, but had failed to pass the entrance examinations. I explained to her why we had to be very careful in making our examinations as stiff as we dared to make them because the benefit and advantage of an appointment to West Point, which gave a fine education, and during which the cadets received a salary from the government, justified a test eliminating the unworthy. She rather impatiently asked me to examine the papers, which I did, and found to my surprise that her son had passed an examination in which he had obtained a mark of 95 out of 100. This was unusual and commended him strongly to me. I found that his rejection had been on the ground that his chest measurement did not bear such a ratio to his height, which was great, as the medical board had thought to be proper and necessary. I explained to the lady the necessity that we were under of having strong and healthy boys educated at West Point, because if there was anything organically the trouble with them which might develop later, the government ran the risk of being obliged to retire such men for disability and to pay them three-fourths pay all their lives without receiving any compensatory service. She listened to this explanation with a lack of attention and a nervous restlessness which husbands will understand. An examination of the papers, however, made me feel that, as we needed men of brains as well as brawn in the army, the unusual mental capacity would justify my running the risk of the boy's filling out his chest measurements to the required extent. I said to the mother therefore that as I had no difficulty in filling out my chest measurement, I thought it would be possible for her son, with his intellectual capacity, to follow a regimen to give his lungs the proper room, and that I was inclined to waive the objections. She did not quite follow me in my statement and she inquired eagerly, "Are you going to let him in?" I said I was, and then there spread over her comely face a rosy smile, and she hesitated a moment to think what she could say to express her gratitude and her satisfaction with me, and then she said, "Mr. Secretary, you are not nearly so fat as they say you are." A recollection of that remark has enabled me to get through a good many scenes that were much more annoying and had a much less satisfactory issue.

The framers of our Constitution had one essential feature of efficient government clearly in mind. They gave to the Executive officer charged in law with the responsibility and actually charged by the people with the responsibility of carrying on the Executive department of the government, the power and means of meeting that responsibility. They vested in him complete power to appoint all the officers of the government who were subordinate to him, and upon whose political capacity and governmental discretion would depend the wise carrying out of his policies. They gave him the power of absolute removal, and they placed in his hands the control of the action of all those who took part in the discharge of the political duties of the executive department. They acted on a sound political principle, and it ought to be introduced into every field of governmental activity, into the states and into the cities. The plan under which a dozen state officers engaged in executing the laws are elected on one ticket and have no relation of subordination to the normal executive head, the governor, is as absurd as it can be. It is one of those anomalies in our political history, of which there are a number, which seem to refute the idea that we are an intelligent and clear-sighted people, because the system adopted is so utterly at variance with the teachings of experience. But we have had such governments—indeed most of our state governments are of this kind. They have not been as good governments as they might have been or as they ought to have been, and yet they have worked. The fact that they have worked, may properly be taken as the most conclusive evidence of the political capacity of the American people through public opinion to maintain a fairly good government and to get along somehow, with what seems *a priori* to be an impossible system. The Constitutional Convention has recommended a change in the present form of the government of New York, which is a most flagrant example in its plan of what a state government ought not to be. They have reduced the number of elective officers to four, on the principle of what is called the short ballot, and they have put the seventeeen departments of the state under the executive control of the governor. This is as it should be, and is a step forward of such notable and radical character that the change that it would make alone is enough to justify the adoption of the proposed Constitution.

4

The Duty of the President to
Take Care that the Laws Are Executed

The Power and Duties of the President as Commander-in-Chief

The widest power and the broadest duty which the President has is conferred and imposed by a clause in section three of article two, providing that "he shall take care that the laws be faithfully executed." This same duty is enforced by the provision that before he enter on the execution of his office, he shall take the following oath or affirmation:

> I do solemnly swear or affirm that I will faithfully execute the office of President of the United States, and will to the best of my ability, preserve, protect and defend the Constitution of the United States.

In executing a statute of Congress, through the proper department and the proper subordinate officers, the President's course is as clear, or as doubtful, as the statute. In order that he or his subordinates shall enforce the statute, they must necessarily find out what it means, and on their interpretation of it enforce the law. Statutory construction is practically one of the greatest of executive powers. Some one has said, "Let me make the ballads of the country, and I care not who makes the laws." One might also say, paraphrasing this, "Let any one make the laws of the country, if I can construe them." Of course ultimately where a statute affects private right, it is likely to come before the courts in actual litigation and to put upon the courts the duty of its construction. But there are many statutes that do not affect private right in such a way that they come under the court's interpretation; and in such cases Executive interpretation is final. Even where it is not, it is very persuasive with courts who subsequently are obliged to adjudge the meaning of the statute.

In the practical provision for the enforcement of law by Congress, that body has found it necessary to impose upon the President or his subordinates not only a purely Executive function, but to enlarge this into what are really quasi-legislative and quasi-judicial duties. Frequently in statutes covering a wide field, Congress confers upon the particular subordinate of the President, who is to execute this law, the power to make rules and regulations under it which are legislative in their nature. This is for the purpose of enabling those who are affected by the terms of the law, both government officers and the public, to learn how it is to be enforced, and how it is to be complied with. If you would know the importance, difficulty and wide discretion involved in such a task, I commend you to the present income tax, and beg you to note "the main strength" that had to be used in formulating workable regulations for its operation and enforcement, and which were really a reconciliation of the parts of the law that seemed inconsistent and almost irreconcilable.

The Commissioner of Internal Revenue, with the approval of the Secretary of the Treasury, issues regulations for the collection of the internal revenue taxes generally. The customs laws are interpreted and supplemented by regulations of the Secretary of the Treasury. The Department of the Interior, in the administration of the land laws, has a book of regulations that are of a minor legislative character, and this is true of other bureaus and departments of the government in respect to laws to be enforced by them.

Congressional legislation often confers on those who comply with its conditions property rights or valuable privileges. Now Congress may exercise a choice as to whether it shall give jurisdiction to pass upon the claims of those seeking these rights to an Executive tribunal or a Judicial tribunal. The application for a patent for an invention is made to the Commissioner of Patents or a subordinate, but provision is made for an appeal from his decision to the Secretary of the Interior and thence to a court. Soldiers' pensions, however, and patents under the homestead and other general land laws for government lands, are granted upon application, after a hearing before an Executive tribunal, to determine whether the applicants come within the conditions of the act granting the pension or the land. Under the immigration acts are officers exercising similar quasi-judicial powers subject to review by the head of the department only, for the purpose of determining whether immigrants who come to this country are eligible under its laws to enter. The laws have now gone to the extent of providing that such tribunals may direct the deportation of those who have illegally entered, and that they may finally decide, after a fair hearing, whether a man claiming to be a citizen of the United States, and thus entitled to enter, is really such a citizen. This shows how judicial in its nature the function of the subordinates of the President in the execution of laws may become.

Then consider the drawing of money from the Treasury Department under an appropriation act. The drawing of the warrant must be approved by the Comptroller of the Treasury. It is for him to say how the appropriation act shall be construed and whether the warrant is lawful and whether the money can be drawn. The Comptroller of the Treasury is an appointee of the President, and in a general sense is his subordinate. If the President does not like him as a Comptroller, he can remove him and with the consent of the Senate put in another one, but under the act of Congress creating the office, the President cannot control or revise the decisions of this officer. His work is like the work I have referred to, quasi-judicial. If the claim is rejected by him, the claimant may in some cases carry his case into the Court of Claims, but if he decides for the claimant, the public and those interested in maintaining the side of the government have no appeal, and his decision is final.

Originally claims against the government could not be heard in court. The government did not permit itself to be sued, the claims were passed upon by Executive officers and were referred to Congress for its consideration and action by appropriation. Now a Court of Claims has been established with jurisdiction to hear and adjudge suits against the United States, based on contracts, express or implied, and in a narrow class of torts. Judgments in the Court of Claims are certified to Congress for payment and are subject to review by the Supreme Court of the United States. This development from the decision of executive officers from claims depending upon government concession or grants, into executive tribunals and finally into a real judicial hearing before a court, is one of numerous instances of the tendencies of the Anglo-Saxon to give a hearing as fair and equitable as is consistent with the effective operation of the government purpose. It was seen originally in the growth and development of the court of chancery out of the arbitrary decisions of the Lord Keeper in dealing with the litigants at common law, and ameliorating its rigidity. The creation of many executive Commissions has given rise to qualms in the minds of some, lest we are departing from those forms of proceeding intended to protect individual right. It may well be pointed out that the trend in all such executive tribunals is toward due judicial hearing and procedure.

The instances that I have been considering are cases of government concession. Of course in such cases it is entirely within the power of Congress to prescribe the conditions of granting the concession. When individuals are affected by act of Congress in their vested rights of life, liberty and property, then Congress is limited in conferring its method. One general limitation is that Congress may not deprive a person of his life, liberty or property except by due process of law. Therefore Congress may not confer on the Executive, judicial power, that is, power to decide cases that according to the due course of law should be heard by courts. Such are controversies of private right between individuals. Such are the trials of individuals for crimes. An executive may not be vested with the authority to decide such issues. This is the general rule, and yet custom and the due course at common law have created exceptions to this general rule, exceptions growing out of the inherent necessities of government. The collection of taxes deprives a man of his property by taking a part of it, but there is no limitation upon the legislative power requiring it to afford judicial settlement of the amount of taxes to be collected from an individual under uniform rules laid down by the legislature. The method must be summary. Congress may vest final decision as to their construction in any executive officer or board. Of course if the tax law violates the Constitution, then it is void and gives no officer any authority to act under it. But where the question is only one of construction, Congress may, in tax cases, keep it out of the courts entirely and vest final interpretation and execution in the taxing officer. Congress has not generally done this, but has ultimately given an opportunity for the taxpayer to appeal to the Federal courts. However, the United States always takes the money first. No injunction is permitted to suspend the agony of an unwilling taxpayer and permit him to withhold the money pending the deliberation of a court.

The express duties defined in the statute, and distributed to the departments and to the various appointees of the President, create a great permanent organization over which he can exercise only a very general supervision. Under the civil service laws, inadequate as they are in some respects, the continuity of the government in the departments at Washington in routine matters is fairly well settled and is little changed from administration to administration. It would he difficult, if the President chose to exercise the power he has, to impose his personality minutely on the going government. He can insist upon greater economy. He can infuse a new spirit in the service by making plain his earnest desire for greater efficiency, and yet while he is, of course, the real head of the government, there seems to be an impersonal entity in the permanent governmental structure, independent of him, which in some degree modifies his responsibility for its operation. Chiefs of Divisions and clerks of Bureaus in the civil service in Washington have been there for decades. They are loyal to the government, and not especially beholden to any one President. They are as important in the army of civil servants as the old non-commissioned officers are in a military force. They have far greater experience than the heads of their departments and bureaus who change every Presidential term. Their life-long fidelity and efficiency are not rewarded by notices in headlines. They have true philosophy, and are content with small salaries, permanent tenure, a conscience of duty well done and the flattering dependence upon them that their immediate superiors manifest. This permanent structure of government works on. Presidents may go to the seashore or to the mountains, Cabinet Officers may go about the country explaining how fortunate the country is in having such an administration, but the machinery at Washington continues to operate under this army of faithful non-commissioned officers, and the great mass of governmental business is uninterrupted. The President notes little of this normal operation of the regular vast machine of government, which in many respects is automatic, unless its workings result in a break or there is a palpable need of repair. The chief concern of the President is in following a path that is not so clearly beaten as the routine work done by this inconspicuous but necessary governmental machine which I have described.

The laws that the President must take care shall be faithfully executed are not confined to acts of Congress. The treaties of the United States with other countries are under the Constitution laws of the United States having the same effect as Congressional enactments, in so far as they are intended to operate in this way and are in form appropriate. Sometimes, however, Congress does not like a treaty and refuses to pass a law to make compliance with it by the Executive as easy at it ought to be. This was the case with the treaty which John Jay made with Great Britain. Jay was hung in effigy, and his work though ratified by the Senate and Washington was nearly as unpopular as the alien and sedition laws of a little later period.

Jay's Treaty provided that England and the United States on proper requisition from each to the other should deliver up all persons charged with murder or forgery, within the jurisdiction of one and seeking an asylum in the jurisdiction of the other. Congress during John Adams' administration passed no law to carry out this article and made no provision, as it has done since in all such cases, for any examination of the accused before a court as the basis for granting a warrant of extradition. No express power was given to the President to issue such a warrant. The matter stood on the naked words of the treaty. A subject of Great Britain committed a murder on the high seas on a British ship, and then escaped to South Carolina. He was there apprehended and brought before the Federal court for commitment on the charge of piracy in alleged violation of statutes of the United States. President Adams wrote to the examining judge that it did not seem to him that this was piracy and that the Federal court had no jurisdiction over the act as such; that the crime was murder and was committed within the jurisdiction of Great Britain and therefore was within the treaty; that the English government had requested the delivery of the accused under the treaty to their agent, and that if the judge found the evidence of the probable guilt of the prisoner sufficient, he, the President, would order him to be turned over to England. The judge agreed that there was no jurisdiction in the Federal court, but said that the evidence was sufficient for commitment on the charge of homicide. The President issued his warrant, the man was delivered to the English authorities and was tried and executed for his offense. Edward Livingston, one of the greatest jurists that ever lived in the United States, was then a Republican member of Congress and a follower of Jefferson, and a very strenuous political opponent of President Adams. He introduced resolutions which recited that the action of the President was an unjustifiable interference with the court's jurisdiction, that there was no statute authorizing an order of extradition by the President, and therefore that his act was a usurpation and a violation of the personal rights of the man who had been extradited and executed. John Marshall, afterwards Chief Justice, was then a member of the House of Representatives and a supporter of the administration. He made an argument to sustain the validity of President Adams' warrant. It is reported in the first appendix of the Fifth Wheaton. Mr. Justice Gray, speaking for the Supreme Court, nearly one hundred years later, pronounced the argument to be masterly and conclusive, and to establish that within the President's constitutional obligation to take care that the laws be faithfully executed, the treaty obligation of the United States was such a law. If you will read the argument of then Congressman Marshall, you will agree with the Court and Mr. Justice Gray. It is as convincing and as judicial in its tone as one of Chief Justice Marshall's great judgments.

A similar instance came within my own official cognizance when I was Secretary of War. In the absence of Mr. Root, Secretary of State, President Roosevelt sent me to Cuba to see if we could compose a revolution against President Palma's government in that Republic. We found a revolution flagrant, and we felt that intervention was necessary, and the question was whether the President, without action of Congress, could use the army and navy and intervene under the so-called Platt Amendment of the Treaty between Cuba and the United States. That Amendment was in part as follows:

> The Government of Cuba consents that the United States may exercise the right to intervene for the preservation of Cuban independence, and the maintenance of a government adequate for the protection of life, property, and individual liberty.

I advised the President that this treaty, *pro tanto,* extended the jurisdiction of the United States to maintain law and order over Cuba in case of threatened insurrection, and of danger of life, property and individual liberty, and that under his duty to take care that the laws be executed this was "a law" and his power to see that it was executed was clear. Events followed quickly our investigation and recommendations, and I was obliged to ask for the army and navy and by authority of President Roosevelt to institute a provisional government, which lasted nearly two years. It restored order and provided a fair election law, conducted a fair election, and turned that government over to the officers elected under the Constitution of Cuba. There were some mutterings by Senators that under the Platt Amendment, Congress only could decide to take action. However, the matter never reached the adoption of a resolution. Congress appropriated the money needed to meet the extraordinary military and naval expenditures required, and recognized the provisional government in Cuba in such a way as to make the course taken a precedent.

Nor are the laws of the execution of which the President is to take care, confined to express Congressional statutes and provisions having force of law in treaties. The Supreme Court has declared that any obligation infer- able from the Constitution, or any duty of the President or the Attorney- General to be derived from the general code of his duties under the laws of the United States is a law within the meaning of this phrase. This was decided in an interesting case from California. Sarah Althea Hill, a resident in California, said she was married to Ex-Senator Sharon of Nevada, and Senator Sharon said she was not. She brought suit in the courts of Califor- nia to secure a divorce, with alimony, to be satisfied out of his very large estate, and made proof of the marriage by introducing a letter purporting to be written by Senator Sharon admitting the marriage. Senator Sharon then went into the Federal Court as a citizen of Nevada, and sued Miss Hill of California to compel her to deliver up this paper purporting to be a letter of his, on the ground that it was false and forged, and that she was using it to his detriment, as she certainly was. In the Federal Court, Mr. Justice Field rendered several decisions adverse to Miss Hill's claims. Meantime, Senator Sharon had died and Miss Hill had married her coun- sel, Judge Terry. When Justice Field was delivering one of his judgments, adverse to Mrs. Terry, Judge and Mrs. Terry were in the court-room, and Mrs. Terry rose and denounced Judge Field and attempted to assault him. He sent her to jail for thirty days. He also sent Judge Terry to jail for assault made by him upon the court bailiffs after Mrs. Terry's arrest. Judge and

Mrs. Terry then and frequently thereafter threatened that when the opportunity came they would kill Judge Field. The Justice returned to Washington to sit upon the Supreme Court and notice of the threats was brought to the attention of Attorney-General Miller. He deemed them serious enough to direct the United States Marshal of California to assign a deputy to accompany Justice Field when he was traveling upon the circuit the next year in California. This was done. After having held court at Los Angeles, Mr. Justice Field was traveling to San Francisco to hold court there. He got out of the train at Lathrop, a station near Fresno, to breakfast. At the same time a train arrived from San Francisco upon which were Judge and Mrs. Terry. Justice Field had entered the restaurant when the Terrys came in and saw him. Mrs. Terry at once returned to her sleeping car to secure a revolver which she had left in her satchel. Judge Terry advanced toward Judge Field, and as the court found, attacked him from behind. Neagle, the Deputy United States Marshal, who was protecting Judge Field, rose, called to Terry that he was an officer, and demanded that he cease his attack. Terry, as Neagle testified, made a movement as if to draw a weapon, and in defense of Justice Field Neagle shot twice and killed Terry. Neagle was indicted in the state court of California for murder for killing Terry. He applied to the Circuit Court of the United States for a writ of *habeas corpus* to discharge him from the custody of the state court, on the ground that the act for which he had been indicted he had committed in pursuance of a law of the United States, and that under the Federal statute giving in such case the right of release by *habeas corpus* by the Federal Courts he was entitled to his discharge. Judge Sawyer, of the Circuit Court, granted Neagle's application and released him. The state of California carried the case to the Supreme Court of the United States. The question was whether in the absence of an express statute giving the President or the Attorney-General of the United States or the United States Marshal the duty and power to protect a United States Judge in the discharge of his duties such protection was an act in pursuance of a law of the United States. The Court likened the word "law" to the term "laws" in the constitutional obligation of the President to take care that the laws of the United States be faithfully executed, and Mr. Justice Miller, speaking for the Court, held that the government of the United States, in view of the constitutional provision for the appointment of Judges and the establishment of a system of courts, was under an obligation to protect its Judges from assault by disappointed litigants when those Judges were in the discharge of their official duties, and that such an obligation constituted a law which it was the duty of the President to take care should be faithfully executed. He said, "It would be a great reproach to the system of government of the United States, declared to be within its sphere, sovereign and supreme, if there is to be found within the domain of its powers no means of protecting its Judges in the conscientious and faithful discharge of their duties from malice and hatred of those upon whom their judgments may operate unfavorably."

Speaking of the injunction upon the President to take care that the laws be faithfully executed, he said, "Is this duty limited to the enforcement of acts of Congress or of treaties of the United States according to their express terms, or does it include the rights, duties and obligation growing out of the Constitution itself, our international relations and all the protection implied by the nature of the government under the Constitution?" He affirms the latter alternative.

He then cites the action of a captain of a United States naval vessel in compelling the surrender in the harbor of Smyrna, by an Austrian vessel, of Kotza, a Hungarian, who had made his declaration of intention to become a citizen of the United States, as an instance in which the Executive enforced "a law" of the United States, not on the statute book, in protecting an "embryo" American citizen against foreign aggression. He instances as analogous cases the action of the President in ordering the army and marshals of the United States to maintain the safety of the mails, and to protect public land from trespassers, all in the interest of the government, and all without express statutory authority so to do.

The same principle seems to be exemplified in Logan against the United States, 144 U. S. 263–284. There a band conspired to kill certain prisoners in the custody of a United States Marshal, and being carried from court to a jail. The prisoners were handcuffed and shackled, and several of them as well as their assailants were killed in the attack. The surviving conspirators were indicted under a statute of the United States punishing a conspiracy to injure or oppress any citizen in the free exercise or enjoyment of "a right then and there secured to him by the Constitution of the United States." Neither the Constitution nor any statute expressly provides for protection of a United States prisoner from assault or conspiracy.

But the Court held that he does have a right under the Constitution to be protected from assault. Mr. Justice Gray, speaking for the Court, said, "In this case the United States having the absolute right to hold prisoners, have an equal duty to protect them while so held against assault or injury from any quarter. The existence of that duty on the part of the government necessarily implied a corresponding right of the prisoner to be so protected and this right of the prisoners is a right secured to them by the Constitution and laws of the United States."

Let me give another example of a law not embodied in a statute or treaty, which, due to Congressional neglect to act, the President has had to see executed.

By an act approved April 28th, 1904, the President was directed to take possession and occupy on behalf of the United States the Canal Zone, the dominion over which had been acquired under the Hay-Varilla Treaty, just then ratified. The seventh section of the act provided "that all the military, civil and judicial powers, as well as the power to make the rules and regulations necessary for the government of the Canal Zone, should be vested in such a person and should be exercised in such a manner as the President should direct until the expiration of the 58th Congress."

When the 58th Congress expired no further provision had been made for the government of the Zone. I was Secretary of War from 1904 to 1908, and in charge of the Canal work. The question arose as to what was to be done in this legislative lapse of government after the death of the 58th Congress. I had no hesitation in advising the President, and I may add he had no hesitation in accepting the advice, that his statutory duty was to build the Canal, and his constitutional duty to take care that the laws be faithfully executed required him to maintain the existing government and continue the *status quo* which was necessary to the construction of the Canal. Congress made no further provision for the government of the Zone for seven years, and by its acquiescence vindicated this view of the President's duty. It is true that one Congressman, now the Governor General of the Philippines, rose in his place in Congress to denounce our usurpation, but except for his lucubration on the subject, no objection was made in Congress and no action was taken. The truth was that Congress did not know exactly what to do and so left it to the President to assume the responsibility.

The President is the Commander-in-Chief of the army and navy, and the militia when called into the service of the United States. Under this, he can order the army and navy anywhere he will, if the appropriations furnish the means of transportation. Of course the instrumentality which this power furnishes, gives the President an opportunity to do things which involve consequences that it would be quite beyond his power under the Constitution directly to effect. Under the Constitution, only Congress has the power to declare war, but with the army and the navy, the President can take action such as to involve the country in war and to leave Congress no option but to declare it or to recognize its existence. This was the charge made against President Polk in beginning the Mexican War. War as a legal fact, it was decided by the Supreme Court in Prize cases, can exist by invasion of this country by a foreign enemy or by such an insurrection as occurred during the Civil War, without any declaration of war by Congress at all, and it is only in the case of a war of our aggression against a foreign country that the power of Congress must be affirmatively asserted to establish its legal existence.

What constitutes an act of war by the land or naval forces of the United States is sometimes a nice question of law and fact. It really seems to differ with the character of the nation whose relations with the United States are affected. The unstable condition as to law and order of some of the Central American Republics seems to create different rules of international law from those that obtain in governments that can be depended upon to maintain their own peace and order. It has been frequently necessary for the President to direct the landing of naval marines from United States vessels in Central America to protect the American consulate and American citizens and their property. He has done this under his general power as Commander-in-Chief. It grows not out of any specific act of Congress, but out of that obligation, inferable from the Constitution, of the government to protect the rights of an American citizen against foreign aggression, as in the Kotza incident, cited by Mr. Justice Miller in the Neagle case. In practice the use of the naval marines for such a purpose has become so common that their landing is treated as a mere local police measure, whereas if troops of the regular army are used for such a purpose, it seems to take on the color of an act of war.

Thus it would be difficult to explain the landing of our army in Vera

Cruz by force, as anything but an act of war to punish the government of Huerta in Mexico for its refusal to render what was deemed by President Wilson as a proper apology for a violation of our international rights in the arrest of some of our sailors. This act was committed before authority was given by Congress, but the necessary authority for it had passed one House and was passing another at the time, and the question as to the right of the Executive to take the action without Congressional authority was avoided by full and immediate ratification.

In Nicaragua in my administration, an insurrection had led to the immurement of American citizens by insurrectos and the threatened destruction of American property. The President of Nicaragua, whom we had recognized and whose Minister we had received, called upon us to protect our own citizens and their property because he was unable to render them the protection which their treaty rights gave them. This led to the landing of marines and quite a campaign, which resulted in the maintenance of law and order and the elimination of the insurrectos. This was not an act of war, because it was done at the request and with the consent of the lawful authorities of the territory where it took place.

As Commander-in-Chief and in taking care that the laws be faithfully executed, President Cleveland sent General Miles to Chicago to remove the obstruction to the passage of the mails and of interstate commerce which Debs at the head of the American Railway Union was effecting by violence and other unlawful means. This was the case where Governor Altgelt sought by protest to keep the army out of Illinois, on the ground that until he or the legislature requested it, the President had no right to send it into the state for the purpose of suppressing disorder. President Cleveland and Attorney-General Olney earned the gratitude of all lovers of peace and good order by the firm stand which they took in this matter and in maintaining what the Supreme Court had so often decided, that every foot of land within the jurisdiction of the United States, whether in a state or territory, or in the District of Columbia, is territory of the United States upon which the laws of the United States can be executed by the President with all the forces which he has at his lawful command; that there is a peace of the United States, a violation of which consists in forcible resistance to Federal laws. Mr. Cleveland did not have to consult Governor Altgelt as to whether he should send an army to Illinois to see that the peace of the

75

United States was preserved and that the Federal laws were faithfully executed there. The full legality of President Cleveland's action in this regard was sustained by the unanimous judgment of the Supreme Court in the Debs case.

The Constitution provides that the United States shall protect each state against invasion and on the application of the Legislature, or of the Executive when the Legislature cannot be convened, against domestic violence; and an early statute of the United States, still in force, provides that on such an application the President may use the militia of any state or the regular army to suppress such insurrection. In the case of Rhode Island as between claimants for the governorship, the court held that it was within the power of the Federal Executive conclusively to determine so far as that court was concerned who was the governor of the state, a result quite analogous to that which enables the President to recognize foreign governments and to bind all other departments of the government by his recognition.

There is, however, a far wider exercise of the authority by the Executive in his capacity as Commander-in-Chief. It was exemplified in and after the Spanish War. Before and after the Treaty of Paris was made with Spain, by which there were left in our possession, as owners, the Philippines and Puerto Rico, and in our custody, as trustees for the people of Cuba, the Island of Cuba, we acquired responsibilities which were met by occupation of those islands and their government by our army and navy. In the case of Cuba, this continued from 1898 until 1903, when the island was turned over to the Cuban Republic. In the case of Puerto Rico this continued from 1898 until the taking effect of the Foraker Act in April, 1900, and in the Philippines from August 13th, 1898, when we took Manila, until March, 1902, when the President was expressly given power to establish a civil government there. During all this interval of Congressional silence, and acquiescence in the action of the President as Commander-in-Chief, he directly, or through his appointed agents, exercised all the executive power and all the legislative power of government in those territories. After suppressing actual disorder, he created a quasi-civil government and appointed an executive, a civil legislature and civil judges, and became the lawgiver of ten millions of people for a period ranging from two years to four. There was nothing new or startling in the principle of this temporary enlargement of his executive functions. Its novelty was in the great volume of power which the circumstances thrust on him and the extent of the responsibilities and the wide discretion which he had to exercise. The validity of such action had been recognized by the Supreme Court in similar cases arising after the Mexican War, when we took over California and New Mexico. The delay of Congress was useful in all these cases. In respect to Puerto Rico, Congress probably acted too quickly, for the Foraker Act, which provided for its government, was made like the usual territorial acts in the United States, and it did not fit quite the civilization to which it was applied in this community of Spanish laws and customs. In the Philippines, under the wise and statesmanlike foresight of Secretary Root the civil government was framed gradually in that country to suit the exigencies. Congress was quite willing to let President McKinley handle the difficult problems until experience should throw light on the situation. When it did act, it ratified everything the President had done and continued under its authority the government which had been initiated and created by the Commander-in-Chief.

There is an instance of Congressional ratification in which I took part that has some humorous features that perhaps would make it of interest to repeat it.

In 1902, while I was Governor of the Philippines, I returned to this country and visited Washington, and had the pleasure of spending thirty days with Mr. Root as his guest. One Sunday afternoon, while we were talking over Philippine matters, he called my attention to the fact that a question had been raised as to the right of the then Philippine Government, without express Congressional authority, to impose duties on goods imported into the Philippines from the United States. These duties had been a source of a large part of the revenues which we used in carrying on the government in the Islands. He said to me, "Now, Taft, we have collected this money, and we have disbursed it, and if there is any doubt about it, we ought to remove that doubt and not be put in the attitude of unlawfully extorting money and expending it for governmental purposes. Therefore, let's draw up a section for the pending Philippine bill, which shall ratify the collection of these duties." Accordingly, we sat down and jointly drafted such a section which was made a part of the Philippine Act, passed in July, 1902, for the government of the Islands. Thereafter a series of suits were brought to recover back the duties collected by the Philippine Government on goods imported from the United States. The total amount sought to be recovered in these suits was about $3,000,000. One of the suits seeking to recover from the United States $100,000, by Warner, Barnes & Company, was brought to a hearing in the Court of Claims and there defeated, on the ground that there was war in the Philippines and the general commanding had the right to levy duties as he chose. The matter of ratification by Congress was not very much considered. The case was carried to the Supreme Court. The Supreme Court reversed the decision and gave judgment for Warner, Barnes & Company for the full $100,000. The question of ratification was summarily considered by the Court, and to the disgust of Mr. Root and myself, the Court held that the clause which we had drafted for the purpose of ratifying the action of the Philippine Government in collecting these duties, was not intended by Congress to effect the very ratification which we sought. The joke was certainly on us. After the opinion of the Court was announced, the counsel for all these claims, who I am advised was very largely interested in their recovery, because his fee was to be a percentage, came to ask me, then Secretary of War, to consent to an entry of the same judgment in all the other suits, which would have amounted to a judgment for $3,000,000 against the government. I felt very indignant over what I regarded as the injustice and inequity of the decision. These claimants had been able to collect the amount of the duties in the prices at which they sold the goods in the Philippines, and now they were seeking to make the government pay twice to them after it had used the money collected to give them a good government. In a somewhat heated conversation with counsel, I expressed my feelings in regard to the judgment of the Court in such a way as to lead him to denounce me as an anarchist and not properly respectful to the judgment of the highest tribunal in the world. I declined utterly to consent to any judgment and notified him of an intention to file an application for a rehearing. Such an application was filed, and to the surprise of counsel, was granted, because the judgment had been a unanimous judgment and it was supposed that a rehearing would never be granted in such a case. The case was then re-argued, and in that hearing the importance of the ratification by Congress was emphasized. We did not succeed in inducing the Court to reverse itself, though we did elicit from the member of the Court writing the opinion that there were some parts of the record that had escaped his attention. Two of the judges dissented from the judgment of the Court. It then occurred to me that if the question turned on ratification, it was not too late to ratify the collections as to all the claims except that one which had passed into judgment. So I went to Mr. Joseph Cannon, the Chairman of the Appropriations Committee of the House, and presented the case to him. I don't think Mr. Cannon has ever done any work more valuable for the government than he did as the watchdog of the Treasury, even though he sometimes had a profane bark. He at once fell in with my suggestion that we have a second clause of ratification which would leave no doubt in the mind of the Court that Congress intended to ratify the collection of the duties in question. I also consulted Mr. Hale, of Maine, who was Chairman of the Committee on Appropriations in the Senate, and enlisted his active cooperation. We had a fight on the floor of the House and the Senate before we succeeded in putting the ratification through. The question then came up again on the second ratification and in that case we secured a majority of the court, Mr. Justice White pronouncing the judgment in favor of the effectiveness of the ratification, and in this way we defeated what I have always regarded as an inequitable claim. Of course those of us who were interested thought that the last judgment was a deliverance of a Daniel come to judgment. I do not say that there is any association between that judgment and the fact that the Judge who pronounced the majority opinion is now the Chief Justice of the United States; but so he is.

5

Foreign Relations

The Pardoning Power

One of the President's most important powers is that which he exercises over our foreign relations. We are just now very much interested in the issues between us and foreign countries. They seem to be dwarfing domestic questions. The greatest war the world ever saw comes close to us. Our attitude as a neutral, and the necessary interference with the commerce between us and belligerents, raises controversies which call for the utmost care in their negotiation and settlement.

It is well to premise what I have to say about the Executive power in such matters by pointing out the exclusive jurisdiction that the Federal government has in dealing with foreign nations. In our domestic matters, the Executive power is divided between the President, the governors of the states, the Legislative power between Congress and the Legislatures of the states, and the Judicial power between the Federal Judiciary and the state courts; but when we come to governmental action with respect to foreign countries, we find that the framers of the Constitution were most careful to vest in the national government complete jurisdiction, and industriously excluded by express prohibition the interference of the states therein. Thus the President and the Senate were given power to make treaties with foreign nations, while all states are expressly forbidden to make them. Congress is given power to regulate foreign commerce, to levy import and tonnage duties, to declare war and to maintain armies and navies for the purpose of carrying on war, to authorize privateers to prey upon the enemy's commerce, to make rules concerning captures on land and water, to make a uniform rule of naturalization, and to denounce and punish offenses against the law of nations, while the states are expressly forbidden to declare war, to grant letters of marque and reprisal, or indeed to maintain a navy or a standing army, or to levy import or tonnage duties. The Federal Courts are given jurisdiction in all cases affecting Ambassadors and other public Ministers and Consuls, and in cases arising between a state or the citizens thereof and foreign states, citizens and subjects; while the President is given the power to appoint Ambassadors, with the advice and consent of the Senate, and to receive Ambassadors from foreign countries, and as Commander-in-Chief of the army and navy to repel invasions and to carry on the war declared by Congress.

The first and most important duty connected with foreign relations that the President has is that of initiating and drafting treaties with foreign nations and submitting them to the Senate for the Senate's advice and consent, and a two-thirds vote of those present is required in the Senate lawfully to advise and consent to a treaty. Originally in the Constitutional Convention, it was proposed that the Senate should appoint Ambassadors and should make treaties; but toward the latter part of the Convention a change was made in this regard, and the power of the President was very much amplified; and in the matter of treaties it was given to him to negotiate them and to ratify and proclaim them. Neither the Senate nor the House, nor both of them together, can compel the President to make a treaty. He has the sole initiative in this regard. Nor is he bound, after he has made a treaty, and the Senate has advised and consented to it, to ratify it and proclaim it, and the treaty does not go into effect until its ratification. There have been many discussions in the Senate over this treaty-making power, and Senators have assumed that the Senate was the more important factor in the making of treaties than the Executive. They have usually in their arguments referred to the fact that Madison moved in the

Convention that the Senate should make the treaties without the intervention of the Executive, and that it was at first adopted. But I am not able to discover why this history of the present constitutional provision should exalt the Senate or make more important its existing power. It is the present text of the fundamental law that determines who shall exercise the powers which it confers, and I do not understand why the function that the Senate performs is any more important or any more sacred than that of the Executive in the making of treaties.

This leads me to refer to the ground upon which two-thirds of the Senate refused to advise and consent to the general arbitration treaties negotiated by Secretary Knox during my administration with England and France. The treaties in effect provided that the countries concerned should submit all questions capable of judicial solution arising between them, which could not be settled by negotiation, to the decision of an arbitral tribunal, and in case of a difference, to submit to a preliminary tribunal the question whether an issue arising was capable of judicial solution and therefore must be arbitrated under the treaty. A number of Senators objected to the effect of these treaties in that they took away from the Senate the power to withhold consent to an arbitration of a future issue and thus prevented the Senate from exercising the constitutional function with which it is charged, of dealing with foreign relations as they arise. It was argued that such a treaty would be delegating to the permanent arbitral court a decision as to our foreign relations which was vested in the Senate, and that it was unconstitutional for the Senate to consent to make such a delegation. This view it seems to me is radically wrong, or else it proves too much. There is no difference in principle between the consent of the Senate that an existing issue between us and a foreign nation shall be settled by arbitration and an agreement that future questions of a defined class shall be so settled. If the submission of a question to arbitration is a delegation to the arbitration tribunal of the power vested in the Senate over our foreign relations, then the Senate has no power to consent to arbitration at all; and yet this it has done since the foundation of the government. But it is said that by delegating to a preliminary tribunal the question whether the issue arising is within the terms of the treaty or not, the Senate is delegating its power. This view is as faulty as the other one. The question whether an issue is arbitrable within the classification of the treaty is a question of the construction of a treaty; and one of the commonest subjects of arbitration is the proper construction of a treaty. Therefore, if the Senate were to consent to abide the judgment of a tribunal in the future as to whether an issue arising between us and a foreign nation is within a class of arbitrable questions described in a treaty, it is only consenting to arbitrate the construction of the treaty when the event occurs which requires construction. This it has done in numerous treaties already.

The Senate is therefore wrong in its view of this matter, if its view is to rest on the limitations of its constitutional powers. If its view rests merely on the question of expediency, that is a different thing, and I do not need to argue that. But I think it is of the utmost importance that every one interested in the establishment of a League of Nations, for the settlement of differences between them by an international court, should realize that the attitude of the Senate upon the point I have been discussing would make it impossible for the United States to become a member of such a League. I am anxious, therefore, in season and out of season, to argue as forcibly as I may the error of the Senate in this regard.

The treaty-making power is a very broad one. Indeed, it is much more important under our Constitution than in any other country that I know. According to our Constitution, a treaty of the United States, in so far as its provisions are in an appropriate form to operate as such, is a law in the United States, exactly as a statute of Congress is a law in the United States. I think I have already invited your attention to the fact that a treaty may repeal a law of Congress if it is inconsistent with it, and that a law of Congress may repeal a treaty. A treaty operates both as a binding contract with a foreign nation and as municipal law. As a contract binding upon both parties, it cannot be made to lose its obligation by a refusal of either country to perform it. It is thus broken, but the party injured by the breach has in international law a right to damages from the party breaking it. If Congress passes a statute inconsistent with the treaty, while it breaks the treaty it repeals it as municipal law. It does not relieve the nation from its moral and international obligation to make good the breach by damages or otherwise, but it does change the law which binds the officers, citizens and others within the governmental jurisdiction of the United States, to comply not with the treaty, but with the law which abrogated it. This was the effect of the decision of the Supreme Court in the Chinese cases. Under our treaty with China certain classes of Chinese were entitled to come into the country. Congress desired to exclude many of the classes thus entitled, and passed a law doing so. The law broke the treaty, but the immigration officers, the courts and all persons within the territorial jurisdiction of the United States were obliged to conform to the act of Congress, and to exclude those Chinese who had the right to come in under the treaty but were forbidden to do so by the subsequent law.

The treaty-making power is in some respects wider than the power of Congress in the enactment of statutes, in this: As between the states and the Federal government, Congressional legislation is limited to a Federal field marked by the powers expressly granted to Congress within the Constitution and those which may be reasonably implied as necessary and proper to the exercise of the express powers. All other powers are exercised by the legislatures of the state within the restrictions of their respective Constitutions. The treaty-making power, however, is dealing with our foreign relations, and when we deal with our foreign relations, we are a nation undivided and presenting a united front. Everything, therefore, that is natural or customarily involved in such foreign relations, a treaty may cover, whether beyond the law-making power of Congress and within the control of state legislatures, or not. Now one of the usual subjects for consideration of a treaty is the rights of the citizens or subjects of one country while resident in, or passing through, the country of the other, to security of life and limb, to the carrying on of business, or to the inheriting of property or its transmission. The subjects of regulating business in a state, the inheritance of property and its transmission are ordinarily within the cognizance of state legislatures and are not within the power of Congress. Yet by a treaty, aliens may be given rights in a state in respect to such matters even though this is at variance with the laws of the state, and to that extent the treaty-making power controls the statute of the state. It makes an exception to the state statute, in favor of the aliens whose rights are defined in the treaty. This has been decided so many times that there is no doubt about the correctness of the view. The Supreme Court has declined to imply the same limitations upon the treaty-making power as the Constitution imposes upon Congressional law-making. It has said that the treaty-making power would not of course reach to changing a form of state government or perhaps parting with state territory, but it has left quite general and undefined the field that it may occupy.

Sometimes the Executive has not made a treaty with a foreign government, but has recommended to Congress the passage of a law, which, with similar action by the other country, constitutes an agreement between them. Thus the statute authorizing reciprocity with Canada, which passed Congress during my administration, relating to the imposition of duties in this country, which was to take effect upon the enactment of a corresponding law in Canada, would, if Canada had passed a similar statute, have constituted an agreement from which each government could withdraw at will. It was not in form a contract or a treaty. So, too, when I was Secretary of War, President Roosevelt sent me to Panama to adjust the relations between the United States and Panama under the Hay-Varilla Treaty. That treaty was very hastily drawn, and many things were left most indefinite, as for instance the boundaries of the Zone at the termini of the Zone. The Zone was not to include the town of Colon or the town of Panama and yet there was no official delimitation in the records of Panama or Colombia of either town. We were to occupy the same bed with the Panamanians, but our half was in the middle. This created in many ways an embarrassing situation, and in some way or other a *modus vivendi* had to be established. The absence of it had caused great irritation and threatened to obstruct the carrying on of the construction of the Canal. I agreed with the President of the Republic upon a plan by which we might comfortably and peaceably take and occupy our half and the people and government of Panama might keep on either side. The plan contained a great many different provisions. I had no power to make a treaty with Panama, but I did have, with the authority of the President, the right to make rules equivalent to law in the Zone. I therefore issued an order directing the carrying out of the plan agreed upon in so far as it was necessary to carry it out on our side of the line, on condition that, and as long as, the regulations to be made by Panama were enforced by that government. This was approved by Secretary Hay and the President and has constituted down until the present day, I believe, the basis upon which the two governments are carried on in this close proximity. It was attacked vigorously in the Senate as a usurpation of the treaty-making power, and I was summoned before a committee in the Senate to justify what had been done. There was a great deal of eloquence over this usurpation of the Senate's prerogative by Mr. Morgan and other Senators, but the *modus vivendi* continued as the practical agreement between the nations for certainly more than seven years, and my impression is that it is still in force in most of its provisions.

The President has a very large authority outside of treaty-making in our foreign relations. He appoints our Ambassadors to other countries, and he receives Ambassadors from them. This gives him necessarily the duty of carrying on foreign negotiations between ourselves and foreign countries. He and he alone is the representative of our nation in dealing with foreign nations. When I say he alone, I mean that it is he to whom the foreign nations look. He has Ambassadors and Ministers and Consuls in other countries, but they only represent him. In receiving foreign Ambassadors and in sending them, he is bound to determine, when there is any dispute, who the lawful government is, to whom he wishes to accredit his Ambassador and from whom he wishes to receive an Ambassador. Therefore in him is necessarily vested the power and duty of recognizing the lawful government of any country. The influence that he can exert in his recognition of a foreign government we have seen illustrated in President Wilson's refusal to recognize Huerta and his announcement that he never would recognize him. We can see the same influence at work at present in behalf of Carranza, whom he has recognized as the *de facto* President against Villa.

The President carries on the correspondence through the State Department with all foreign countries. He is bound in such correspondence to discuss the proper construction of treaties. He must formulate the foreign policies of our government. He must state our attitude upon questions constantly arising. While strictly he may not bind our government as a treaty would bind it, to a definition of its rights, still in future discussions foreign Secretaries of other countries are wont to look for support of their contentions to the declarations and admissions of our Secretaries of State in other controversies as in a sense binding upon us. There is thus much practical framing of our foreign policies in the executive conduct of our foreign relations.

One of the most important strokes in our international history was the correspondence carried on by Secretary Hay under President McKinley in the establishment of the policy of the open door in China and equal facilities for all nations in dealing with that important empire. That policy was stated in a note by Secretary Hay and acquiesced in by all the nations concerned, and that without any advice and consent of the Senate.

Whenever our American citizens have claims to present against a foreign nation, they do it through the President by the State Department; and when foreign citizens have claims to present against us, they present them through their diplomatic representatives to our State Department, and the formulation and the discussion of the merits of those claims create an important body of precedents in our foreign policy.

The importance of the President in our foreign relations, when his power in that regard is considered in connection with his duty to take care that the laws are faithfully executed, and with his duty as Commander-in-Chief to direct the movements of the Army and Navy, may be noted in the authority which President McKinley exercised to take part in the so-called "Boxer War," in China. The lawless uprising in that ancient Empire against foreigners, which for the time being overthrew the power of the Imperial Government, exposed to danger the lives of the diplomatic representatives of foreign nations at Pekin, and brought about the murder of one of them. Uniting with other governments, President McKinley, without express Congressional authority, ordered the land and naval forces of the United States into a campaign to rescue the foreign legations which were besieged in Pekin.

There has always been a dispute as to whether the treaty-making power can bind Congress to the obligation of a treaty, so that if a treaty provides for the payment of money, Congress is under an obligation to appropriate the money. Of course a treaty may not take money out of the Treasury of the United States, because under the Constitution that can only be taken out by Congress, but it has always seemed to me that while Congress in appropriating money for any purpose exercises its discretion, in that it has the actual power to pay or not to pay, it is bound in honor to perform the contract which the government of the United States has made through that agency appointed by the Constitution to make the contract. When Congress in its discretion, as the appropriating branch of the government, refuses to appropriate the money which the treaty-making power has agreed shall be paid it is merely violating the plighted faith of the government. Just so, it may abrogate a treaty obligation by statute, but it does not annul the obligation. It is exercising the same power that a man has to refuse to pay his note after he has made it through an authorized agent. The man can be compelled to pay his note. Congress may not be compelled because of its exercising the functions of sovereignty, but its failure to act does not destroy its obligation.

The President may not annul or abrogate a treaty without the consent of the Senate unless he is given that specific authority by the terms of the treaty. The ending of a treaty is to be effected by the same power which made the treaty. An instance in my own experience of annulling a treaty comes to me. We had a treaty with Russia proclaimed in 1832. It was a treaty of commerce and friendship. It gave to our merchants certain rights in Russia in carrying on business. Russia refused to extend the rights assured to our merchants to Jews, on the ground that Jews in Russia were limited in their commercial activities and were obliged to carry them on within a pale in that country, and that when our merchants being Jews sought to avail themselves of the privileges of the treaty, they were either denied admission or were subjected to the local laws of Russia and were limited as their coreligionists were limited in Russia. From the time that the question was mooted the two countries had differed as to construction. A similar question had arisen between France and Russia and between England and Russia, but Russia had always insisted upon maintaining the position I have described. The attitude so contrary to our notions of equity and tolerance to all religions naturally irritated our people and led to the introduction of a resolution in the House of Representatives, during my administration, calling upon the President to annul the treaty in accordance with its terms by a year's notice, on the ground that Russia had flagrantly violated its obligations. The resolution was drawn in language which would have given diplomatic offense to Russia, as doubtless its framers intended to do. With the responsibility of maintaining as friendly relations as possible with all the world, it seemed to me that if the treaty had to be abrogated, it ought to be done as politely as possible, with the hope of negotiating a treaty less subject to dispute, and giving more satisfactory result. With the knowledge that the resolution was sure to pass the Senate, I took the step of annulling the treaty myself and giving a year's notice to Russia of the annulment in proper and courteous expressions, on the ground that we had differed so radically as to its construction and the treaty was so old that it would be wiser to make a new treaty more definite and satisfactory. I sent notice of this annulment at once to the Senate, and in this way succeeded in having the Senate substitute a resolution approving my action for the resolution which came over from the House. The House was thus induced to approve my action and the incident was closed for the time. I regret to say that no new treaty has yet been made and our relations with Russia in many regards are defined only by the rules of international law.

The Supreme Court recognizes the power of the President to decide the question of our foreign relations which it calls political, and holds itself bound by the President's action. Early in our history the question arose whether the Falkland Islands belonged to Buenos Aires, so that Buenos Aires might pass a law punishing the killing of seals in those Islands. Our State Department, in correspondence with the government of Buenos Aires, had refused to recognize its lawful jurisdiction there. In a maritime insurance case, the issue was whether a vessel lost through seizure by the authorities of Buenos Aires for violation of its sealing laws was a loss within a marine insurance policy, or was excepted because the master had violated the statutes of a lawful government. The Supreme Court held that it would follow the decision of the President as the political department having the authority to decide such an issue. The Court reached a similar conclusion in another seal case where we were on the other side. Mr. Blaine, as Secretary of State for Mr. Harrison, had claimed in a correspondence with Lord Salisbury that through the grant of Alaska and the adjoining waters we were given jurisdiction over the open Bering Sea to arrest Canadian sealers engaged in pelagic sealing contrary to the laws of the United States. Mr. Blaine's claim was that Russia had asserted territorial jurisdiction over these waters, and that this jurisdiction had been acquiesced in by the world. The Supreme Court intimated in its opinion that this was a political question, and that it would not undertake to discuss the merits of Mr. Blaine's contentions, because it was bound to follow and respect the attitude of the President and Secretary of State in deciding such a question. Of course the decision of Congress or the treaty making power upon such an issue would be binding upon the Courts, but in the absence of the decision of either the action of the President is conclusive with the Courts.

The last power of the President which I shall consider is the power of pardon. This is a wide power, and enables the President to pardon any one guilty of an offense against the United States before indictment, after indictment and before conviction, or after conviction. He need not name the persons to be pardoned if he pardons a class and makes provision by which the persons affected shall establish their membership in that class. The pardon under such circumstances is called an amnesty. He is expressly given power to grant reprieves, which means only a suspension of the execution of a sentence for one purpose or another. The Supreme Court said in one case that a pardon reaches both the punishment prescribed for the offense and the guilt of the offender, and when the pardon is full, it relieves the punishment and blots out of existence the guilt, so that in the eye of the law the offender is as innocent as if he never had committed the offense. This is rather a strong statement as some later cases show. It is difficult to clothe Omnipotence with such a power.

Congress may not restrict the President in the exercise of his power of pardon. There was a good deal of conflict between the Executive and Congress in respect to amnesty proclamations issued by President Johnson. Congress was loath to allow the full constitutional effect which such pardons required in respect to the status of those who had been guilty of treason against the government and who were restored to the enjoyment of their full civil rights, as if the treason had never been committed. In the case of Mr. Garland, who was afterwards a Senator from Arkansas, and Attorney-General of the United States, the Supreme Court had to examine the validity of a statute, which required that every attorney practising law in the Federal court must take an oath that he never had borne arms against the United States. This act practically excluded all lawyers who had served the Confederacy from the pursuit of their profession. The Court held the act invalid because it was in effect a bill of attainder, and also because it defeated the President's amnesty of which Mr. Garland had taken advantage. A very nice line of distinction is presented by another decision of the Supreme Court, in which the validity of a law of the state of New York was in question. The law prevented men who had been convicted of felonies from receiving certificates permitting them to practise medicine. In that case, the Court held that the question of fitness was one of fact and that the legislature had the right to make rules of eligibility to protect the public against immorality in the practise of the profession, and that it could not say that such a rule of ineligibility was not reasonable in preserving a proper moral standard in physicians. It could not regard it as additional punishment.

There is a question whether the President's power of pardons extends to the case of one sentenced to imprisonment for contempt by a Federal Court. It is objected that this power of contempt is used by the court to enforce its judgments, and that if the President could intervene and paralyze the instrument in the hands of the Court to enforce its judgment, he would not be pardoning a crime but would be obstructing the Court in its administration of justice. I think it is possible to smooth out this difficulty by pointing out a distinction between the two ways in which a court exercises its power of contempt. Where a court is seeking to enforce a decree or a judgment against a contumacious party and puts him in prison for the purpose of compelling him to comply with the judgment or decree, then I do not think the President could pardon a man or relieve him from the effect of such an order because he would really be obstructing the cause of justice. But where the court is merely vindicating its own authority by punishing a man for a past contempt, and where an imprisonment is not a continuing duress for the purpose of compelling obedience, it seems to me that the punishment inflicted is for an offense against the United States, to wit, a defiance of its judicial authority, and therefore that it does come within the range of the power of pardon by the President.

The duty involved in the pardoning power is a most difficult one to perform, because it is so completely within the discretion of the Executive and is lacking so in rules or limitations of its exercise. The only rule he can follow is that he shall not exercise it against the public interest. The guilt of the man with whose case he is dealing is usually admitted, and even if it is not, the judgment of the court settles that fact in all but few cases. The question which the President has to decide is whether under peculiar circumstances of hardship he can exercise clemency without destroying the useful effect of punishment in deterring others from committing crimes. The frequent result of human punishment is that those near to the criminal or dependent upon him suffer more than he does, and their pitiable condition often furnishes a plea for mitigation of the penalty to the offender. Those who plead for pardon are generally entirely blind to the right of society to be protected from criminals and to have those of criminal tendencies deterred from yielding to them by fear of punishment. If the fear of punishment is lessened by Executive clemency to those convicted, the benefit of punishment will be largely lost. It is a case where organized emotion and sentiment are likely to mislead, to the public detriment. It seems to me that the people of New York and of the country generally are in danger of being led by an unwise sentiment into a treatment of convicted criminals that will neither impart to the criminals the proper lesson from punishment, nor will keep before those likely to become criminals the fear of the law as a deterrent. It is of course wise and humane that state prisons and penitentiaries should be made as healthful as possible for the confinement of those sentenced to spend a term within their walls, and it is wise to provide healthful labor and primary and industrial education. The impulse of many prison reformers, however, to treat the prisoners as victims and to make society the scapegoat for all their sins and vicious propensities and crimes is a wrong one, which if yielded to will certainly lead to bad results and ultimately to a retracing of steps toward greater rigidity and severity. The theory that by treating criminals as if they had no criminal tendencies you can eliminate such tendencies is one that may work in some cases, but the exceptions will be so many as to make the policy ultimately ridiculous, and, worse than ridiculous, most harmful. A man who violates the law in such a way as to call for a sentence and imprisonment is punished for his violation, and he ought to be punished. He need not be, and ought not to be, subjected to cruel or unwholesome surroundings, but he should be made to feel that he is suffering punishment for that which he has done. He may be given an opportunity to reform, and, so far as it is possible, be encouraged to change his ways, but if he is to be coddled and to receive the impression that he is a victim instead of being a criminal, the enforcement of our criminal law will be a failure.

The President has to keep these distinctions in mind in the exercise of Executive clemency, and must stifle his emotions of pity for the family and dependents of the criminal in the consideration of the character of the offense and the necessity for having it plainly understood that such an offender is not to escape with immunity.

There has been a custom in the Presidential office of pardoning men who are supposed to be near their death to enable them to go home and die with their families. The difficulty in such cases is in being certain that death is near. I had two notable cases in which I was assured by the prison authorities that death was imminent, and that if they were to be released at all, to die, they ought to be released at once. I instituted as thorough an investigation as I could through the army and navy surgeons in the employ of the government and reached the conclusion from the evidence submitted that death was certain. I pardoned them both. One man died and kept his contract. The other recovered at once, and seems to be as healthy and active as any one I know. I had a suspicion of fraud in the latter case and instituted an investigation to see whether I had been deceived by the friends of the prisoner or the prisoner himself. I was not able to find the evidence of such fraud.

It has been suggested to me that if the man had been guilty of fraud in inducing me to pardon him, I might have set aside the pardon as void and directed the arrest of the former convict. I do not think that in such a case a pardon could be set aside. I do not think either I or a court would have had the authority to issue a warrant for the arrest of the man and to restore him to prison. It seems to me it would be like a case of a man acquitted by a jury which was bribed by him. He might be thereafter convicted of bribery, but he could not be convicted of the crime of which the verdict of the jury acquitted him.

There are curious notions about pardons in the minds of some people. When Mr. Knox was Attorney-General, a Congressman came to him and said that he would like to have a man pardoned who had been sent to the penitentiary for robbing a post office. He said that the convict had been a great supporter of his and he would like to get him out. Mr. Knox asked him what the ground for pardon was, and he said he was a good fellow and had been his friend. Knox said that was no reason. "But,"said the Congressman, "I understand that each Congressman has a right to two pardons during his term and I want this to be one of mine."

6

The Limitations of the President's Powers

I have considered, at possibly too great length, the chief powers of the Executive under the Federal Constitution. In theory, the Executive power and the Legislative power are independent and separate, but it is not always easy to draw the line and to say where Legislative control and direction to the Executive must cease, and where his independent discretion begins. In theory, all the Executive officers appointed by the President directly or indirectly are his subordinates, and yet Congress can undoubtedly pass laws definitely limiting their discretion and commanding a certain course by them which it is not within the power of the Executive to vary. Fixing the method in which Executive power shall be exercised is perhaps one of the chief functions of Congress. Indeed, by its legislation, it often creates a duty in the Executive which did not before exist. Then in prescribing how that duty is to be carried out, it imposes restrictions that the Executive is bound to observe.

Congress may repose discretion in appointees of the President, which the President may not himself control. The instance I have already given is one of these, in which the Comptroller of the Treasury has independent quasi-judicial authority to pass on the question of what warrants are authorized by appropriation acts to be drawn by him on the funds of the Treasury. The President can appoint him and remove him, but he may not control him in his construction of appropriation acts and his signing, or withholding his signature from warrants in accordance with that construction.

So, too, as between a court directing the action of a marshal and a contrary order of the President, the marshal is bound by law to follow the court's direction. Indeed, the court may compel him to do so by punishing him for contempt if he refuses to obey the order. If the marshal is obstructed in the performance of his duty, however, and he or the court calls upon the President to send the army to overcome the obstruction, the President cannot be compelled to act.

Two principles, limiting Congressional interference with the Executive powers, are clear. *First,* Congress may not exercise any of the powers vested in the President, and *second,* it may not prevent or obstruct the use of means given him by the Constitution for the exercise of those powers.

In the matter of appointments, Presidents have been quick to resent encroachments by Congress. The power of appointment is not in Congress. In the case of Fitz John Porter, President Arthur made a precedent which prevails. Porter had been sentenced by court-martial for his alleged misconduct in failing to support Pope in the second battle of Bull Run. Twenty years after the court-martial, when Porter's friends were in the majority of Congress, they passed an act authorizing the President to appoint Porter a colonel in the regular army, and to place him on the retired list. President Arthur vetoed the bill, and one of the grounds he gave was that it was an encroachment on the Executive power to make the creation of an office conditioned on the appointment of a named individual. When General Grant was dying at Mt. McGregor, Congress, in response to a throb of sympathy and gratitude throughout the nation, wished to have him put on the retired list as a full general, but when the act was drafted and passed, it did not mention General Grant's name. It merely provided that from among the living Commanding Generals, the President might nominate one, and with the consent of the Senate appoint him to be a general on the retired list, with full pay. The act was passed, General Grant was appointed and confirmed to be a general, with full salary, and the last three months of his life were cheered by this evidence of the continued gratitude of his countrymen.

While Congress may not exercise the power of appointment, it may certainly impose rules of eligibility within which appointees are to be selected. The extent of the right of the President to make appointments, without Congressional control or limitation, has been very recently mooted. An army officer, who was under the statute regulating promotion in the army entitled to a promotion to a vacancy, was not a man whom the President thought ought to be promoted, although he was not subject to removal by a court-martial. He therefore passed him over and nominated the next officer in rank to the vacancy. The then Attorney-General rendered an opinion that the President could not be limited in his appointment of army officers by rules as to promotion in the army contained in the army organization act. I am not aware of what action the Senate has taken. Attempt was made by some proceeding in court to prevent the passing over the officer first entitled, but the jurisdiction of the court to control the Executive evidently could not be maintained. If Congress may not provide by law a rule of eligibility for promotion in the army or navy, or if the President may refuse to conform to such a law, it is difficult to see how Congress can exercise the power which it is given by the Constitution to raise and support armies and make rules for the government and regulation of the land and naval forces. Rules of eligibility for promotion would seem to be rules for the regulation of army forces. No court and no other authority, however, can compel the President to make a nomination, and the only method of preventing his appointing someone other than the one specified by law is for the Senate to refuse to confirm him, or for Congress to withhold an appropriation of his salary, or for the Comptroller of the Treasury to decline to draw a warrant for his salary on the ground of his ineligibility under the law. The question of his salary then might be referred to the Court of Claims through a suit by him, and in that way the judgment of the Court might be invoked upon the validity of the appointment. This, however, is one of the numerous instances in which for practical purposes the Constitution is finally construed by the President and the Senate.

The President is made Commander-in-Chief of the army and navy by the Constitution evidently for the purpose of enabling him to defend the country against invasion, to suppress insurrection and to take care that the laws be faithfully executed. If Congress were to attempt to prevent his use of the army for any of these purposes, the action would be void. During the existence of the Federal election laws, there was a provision enacted by Congress forbidding marshals to call upon the army as a *posse comitatus* to assist them in the enforcement of the election laws, but that was not interfering with the President's power as Commander-in-Chief. Under another section of the statute, the President has the power to call upon the army, after proclamation, to resist forcible obstruction of any Federal laws. In other words, he is to maintain the peace of the United States. I think he would have this power under the Constitution even if Congress had not given him express authority to this end. Again, in the carrying on of war as Commander-in-Chief, it is he who is to determine the movements of the army and of the navy. Congress could not take away from him that discretion and place it beyond his control in any of his subordinates, nor could they themselves, as the people of Athens attempted to, carry on campaigns by votes in the market-place.

The President is required by the Constitution from time to time to give to Congress information on the state of the Union, and to recommend for its consideration such measures as he shall judge necessary and expedient, but this does not enable Congress or either House of Congress to elicit from him confidential information which he has acquired for the purpose of enabling him to discharge his constitutional duties, if he does not deem the disclosure of such information prudent or in the public interest. In the controversy between Washington and Congress, over the performance of the Jay Treaty by payment of money, Congress attempted to secure from Washington the correspondence had between him and Chief Justice Jay, and other correspondence about the treaty on the files of the State Department. Washington maintained that the House of Representatives, which was seeking the information, was not part of the treaty-making power and therefore had no right to secure from him confidential information in respect to the making of the treaty which he did not deem wise to make public. He therefore declined to furnish the correspondence, although the House of Representatives adopted resolutions to protest against his action. The House did, however, appropriate the money stipulated for in the treaty.

In the last days of Grant's administration, when the House was Democratic, and when President Grant was being criticized for spending some of the hot months at Long Branch, the House of Representatives sent him a resolution asking for information as to how many Executive acts were performed at other places than the seat of government. The inquiry evidently aroused the General, for his declination to furnish the information is quite spirited. He declined to admit that under the Constitution he was obliged to perform official acts at the seat of government, and proceeded to show by historical reference that many such acts by former Presidents had been performed at other places in the United States. He filed a statement of the time spent at the seat of government by each President, from which it appeared that the President who was most often absent from Washington and the seat of government was Thomas Jefferson, a full quarter of whose time was spent at Monticello. This seemed a very complete answer to the Democratic majority of the House which in passing the resolution were seeking to make political capital, for they could hardly criticize General Grant for doing that which Mr. Jefferson, the founder of the Democratic Party, had done with even more freedom. A visit to his beautiful country seat at Monticello and a knowledge of the very uncomfortable quarters that he had at the White House in the beginnings of our national capital, may explain why Jefferson went to Monticello whenever he could get away from Washington. More than this, he was a great letter writer, and he could write letters as well from Monticello as he could from the White House. I am glad to say that a more reasonable view is now taken of the right of the President to enjoy a vacation at the seashore or in the mountains, whenever he can be spared from Washington, and it is most satisfactory to those of us who have enjoyed some relief of this kind to know that we have Jefferson's conduct to justify us.

Mr. Jefferson set another example which has constituted a precedent never departed from. In the trial of Aaron Burr for treason, Chief Justice Marshall presided in Richmond, and at the instance of the parties to the suit, he directed a subpœna *duces tecum* to be served on President Jefferson, requiring him to bring with him papers supposed to bear on the issue. Mr. Jefferson wrote a letter to the District Attorney declining to respond to the subpœna, and gave as his reason for doing so that he could not be detained as a witness in a case, because it would interfere with his public duties. To this Chief Justice Marshall responded that apparently all his time was not taken up with governmental duties, which Mr. Jefferson construed to mean a reference to the fact that he spent a great deal of his time at Monticello, and an intimation that he might just as well come to Richmond and testify as to go to Monticello and enjoy his leisure. Mr. Jefferson resented the intimation with all the emphasis and vehemence that Chief Justice Marshall's rulings in political and personal matters usually evoked. No other President, so far as I know, has been subpœnaed to appear in court during his term. General Grant did testify in the criminal case brought against Mr. Babcock, his Secretary, in behalf of the defendant. The deposition was given in the White House and was taken before Chief Justice Waite, and in the presence of the Attorney-General.

The Supreme Court seems to make a broad distinction between issuing process against the President and against his subordinates under laws requiring the specific performance of a definite act. I cannot think that the Court would ever issue a mandamus to compel the President to perform even an act purely ministerial, though it has often issued such a writ against one of his subordinates. The Supreme Court has a number of times intimated that the President's office is of such a high character, that officially he is beyond the compulsory processes of the Court. Thus in the case of Mississippi against Johnson, where it was sought by the state of Mississippi to enjoin President Johnson from carrying out the reconstruction acts, on the ground that they were unconstitutional, the Court refused to issue the writ on two grounds, first that it did not have the power to enforce a writ of injunction against the President, who might decline to obey its writ, and second on the ground that the unconstitutionality of such an act directing an executive officer with respect to the government of a state was a political question which it could not control, but which must be decided by the executive to whose discretion the enforcement of the act was entrusted.

As already said, the court has always fully conceded its duty to recognize, as binding upon it, the political powers exercised by the Executive and Legislative departments of the government under the Constitution. It is not always easy to say what is a political issue. Possibly the latest case of this kind is the one in which a corporation sought to evade the payment of taxes in Oregon, on the ground that the law under which they were exacted had been passed by an initiative and a referendum. It was contended that an initiative and referendum were inconsistent with a republican form of government as understood by the framers of the Constitution, and as the United States guaranteed to each state a republican form of government, such a method of legislation must be invalid and no taxes could be collected under it. The Supreme Court answered that the question whether a state had a republican form of government was a political question for Congress to settle, and that as long as Congress continued to recognize Oregon as a state, it was not for the Court to investigate the question. I think myself that there is no doubt that the term "republican" in that clause in the Constitution was intended to distinguish our kind of government from a monarchical form, and that it was not intended to make a distinction between what is called a republican form of government and a purely democratic or direct form of popular government. Congress is the authority to decide this question, and it has already so decided it in the cases of Oklahoma, of Arizona, and of New Mexico, because the constitutions of those states containing provisions for the initiative and the referendum were before it and were approved.

An instance of how the Legislative and Executive departments can decide a constitutional question without the intervention of Congress may be seen in the appropriation made by one Congress during the Spanish-American War of $3,000,000, to be expended through the War Department with the approval of the President for contingencies that could not be foreseen. This fund was not completely expended for some four or five years after the appropriation. It was a very useful fund, as I can testify, because it enabled us in the administration of the Philippines to meet extraordinary expenses which had to be incurred in the suppression of the insurrection, in the detection of sedition, in the encouragement of friendly relations with the people and in many other ways. The point was made by one member of the appropriation committee that this was an appropriation in support of the army, and therefore must be limited by the Constitution to two years, but the view of the department and of the Comptroller of the Treasury was that this appropriation was not included within the limitation because it was not for the support of the army and was not used therefor, although included in the Army Appropriation Bill expended by the War Department in the suppression of the disorders in the Philippines and in Cuba.

Executive power is sometimes created by custom, and so strong is the influence of custom that it seems almost to amend the Constitution. Take the case of Postal Treaties. The Constitution says that treaties with foreign governments shall be made by the President, by and with the advice of a two-thirds vote of the Senate; and yet postal arrangements in the nature of treaties had been made between this country and the European countries before the Constitution was adopted, and continued to be made after its adoption, without Senate action, until 1844 when the one postal treaty that was ever made in that way was signed by the President and consented to by the Senate. Almost immediately thereafter Congress passed an act which authorized the Postmaster-General to make treaties affecting postal matters, with postal authorities of other countries, subject to the consent of the President, and this is an exception grafted on to the Constitution merely through Executive practice. A similar case is that of the remission of penalties incurred by steamers violating the navigation laws. Since the beginning of the government, the Secretary of the Treasury has exercised the power to remit these penalties in proper cases. The pardoning power is given by the Constitution to the President, yet the practice of one hundred years was recognized by the Supreme Court and it was held to be valid.

In a very recent case, in which President Roosevelt had exercised the power to withdraw lands, which were open for settlement under an act of Congress, from the operation of the act, and in which course I had followed him with very considerable doubt as to my power, the validity of our action was brought before the Supreme Court and sustained, on the ground that the practice of the Executive for a great many years, with the acquiescence of Congress in such withdrawals, justified the exercise of the power and made it legal as if there had been an express act of Congress authorizing it.

One of the great questions that the Executive has had to meet in the past has been how far he might properly differ from the Supreme Court in the construction of the Constitution in the discharge of his duties. Jefferson, in a letter to Mrs. John Adams, laid it down with emphasis with reference to the Sedition Law, in which he said:

The Judges, believing the law constitutional, had a right to pass a sentence of fine and imprisonment, because the power was placed in their hands by the Constitution. But the executive, believing the law to be unconstitutional, might remit the execution of it, because that power has been confided to them by the Constitution. That instrument meant that its coordinate branches should be checks on each other. But the opinion which gives to the Judges the right to decide what laws are constitutional, and what not, not only for themselves in their own sphere of action, but for the legislature and executive also, in their spheres, would make the judiciary a despotic branch.

And so Jackson in his message vetoing the renewal of the charter to the bank of the United States in respect to the opinion of the Supreme Court confirming the constitutionality of the previous charter, said:

If the opinion of the Supreme Court covered the whole ground of this act, it ought not to control the coordinate authorities of this Government. The Congress, the Executive and the Court must each for itself be guided by its own opinion of the Constitution. Each public officer who takes an oath to support the Constitution swears that he will support it as he understands it, and not as it is understood by others. It is as much the duty of the House of Representatives, of the Senate, and of the President to decide upon the Constitutionality of any bill or resolution which may be presented to them for passage or approval as it is of the Supreme judges when it may be brought before them for judicial decision. The opinion of the judges has no more authority over Congress than the opinion of Congress has over the judges, and on that point the President is independent of both. The authority of the Supreme Court must not, therefore, be permitted to control the Congress or the Executive when acting in their legislative capacities, but to have only such influence as the force of their reasoning may deserve.

Mr. Lincoln in his reference to the Dred Scott case said:

I do not forget the position assumed by some that constitutional questions are to be decided by the Supreme Court, nor do I deny that such decisions must be binding in any case upon the parties to a suit as to the object of that suit, while they are also entitled to very high respect and consideration in all parallel cases by all other departments of the Government. And while it is obviously possible that such decision may be erroneous in any given case, still the evil effect following it, being limited to that particular case, with the chance that it may be overruled and never become a precedent for other cases, can better be borne than could the evils of a different practice. At the same time, the candid citizen must confess that if the policy of the Government upon vital questions affecting the whole people is to be irrevocably fixed by decisions of the Supreme Court, the instant they are made in ordinary litigation between parties in personal actions the people will have ceased to be their own rulers, having to that extent practically resigned their government into hands of that eminent tribunal. Nor is there in this view any assault upon the court or the judges. It is a duty from which they may not shrink to decide cases properly brought before them, and it is no fault of theirs if others seek to turn their decisions to political purposes.

I do not intend to dispute the attitude of these distinguished men. Nor is it necessary to do so. It is sufficient to say that the Court is a permanent body, respecting precedent and seeking consistency in its decisions, and that therefore its view of the Constitution, whether binding on the Executive and the legislature or not, is likely ultimately to prevail as accepted law.

While it is important to mark out the exclusive field of jurisdiction of each branch of the government, Legislative, Executive and Judicial, it should be said that in the proper working of the government there must be cooperation of all branches, and without a willingness of each branch to perform its function, there will follow a hopeless obstruction to the progress of the whole government. Neither branch can compel the other to affirmative action, and each branch can greatly hinder the other in the attainment of the object of its activities and the exercise of its discretion. The judicial branch has sometimes been said to be the most powerful branch of the government because in its decision of litigated cases it is frequently called upon to mark the limits of the jurisdiction of the other two branches. As already noted, by its continuity and the consistency of its decisions, the Court exercises much greater power in this regard than the other two branches. But it has no instruments to enforce its judgments, and if the Executive fails to remove the obstructions that may be offered to the execution of its decrees and orders, when its authority is defied, then the Court is helpless. It may not directly summon the army or the navy to maintain the supremacy of the law and order. So if the judges of the Court were to refuse to perform the judicial duties imposed by Congress, the object of Congress in much of its legislation might be defeated. And if Congress were to refuse to levy the taxes and make the appropriations which are necessary to pay the salaries of government officials, and to furnish the equipment essential in the performance of their duties, it could paralyze all branches of the government. The life of the government, therefore, depends on the sense of responsibility of each branch in doing the part assigned to it in the carrying on of the business of the people in the government, and ultimately as the last resource, we must look to public opinion as the moving force to induce affirmative action and proper team work. The power over the purse is, however, practically the greatest power, and that Congress exercises without control by either of the other branches. Therefore when fear is expressed of the usurpation by other branches and the thieving of jurisdiction by either, we must keep in mind that the legislative power to withhold appropriations is that which in the history of constitutional government has always been the most powerful agency in the defense of the people's rights.

The true view of the Executive functions is, as I conceive it, that the President can exercise no power which cannot be fairly and reasonably traced to some specific grant of power or justly implied and included within such express grant as proper and necessary to its exercise. Such specific grant must be either in the Federal Constitution or in an act of Congress passed in pursuance thereof. There is no undefined residuum of power which he can exercise because it seems to him to be in the public interest, and there is nothing in the Neagle case and its definition of a law of the United States, or in other precedents, warranting such an inference. The grants of Executive power are necessarily in general terms in order not to embarrass the Executive within the field of action plainly marked for him, but his jurisdiction must be justified and vindicated by affirmative constitutional or statutory provision, or it does not exist. There have not been wanting, however, eminent men in high public office holding a different view and who have insisted upon the necessity for an undefined residuum of Executive power in the public interest. They have not been confined to the present generation. We may learn this from the complaint of a Virginia statesman, Abel P. Upshur, a strict constructionist of the old school, who succeeded Daniel Webster as Secretary of State under President Tyler. He was aroused by Story's commentaries on the Constitution to write a monograph answering and criticizing them, and in the course of this he comments as follows on the Executive power under the Constitution:

> The most defective part of the Constitution beyond all question, is that which related to the Executive Department. It is impossible to read that instrument, without being struck with the loose and unguarded terms in which the powers and duties of the President are pointed out. So far as the legislature is concerned, the limitations of the Constitution, are, perhaps, as precise and strict as they could safely have been made; but in regard to the Executive, the Convention appears to have studiously selected such loose and general expressions, as would enable the President, by implication and construction either to neglect his duties or to enlarge his powers. *We have heard it gravely asserted in Congress that whatever power is neither legislative nor judiciary, is of course executive, and, as such, belongs to the President under the Constitution.* How far a majority of that body would have sustained a doctrine so monstrous, and so utterly at war with the whole genius of our government, it is impossible to say, but this, at least, we know, that it met with no rebuke from those who supported the particular act of Executive power, in defense of which it was urged. Be this as it may, it is a reproach to the Constitution that the Executive trust is so ill-defined, as to leave any plausible pretense even to the insane zeal of party devotion, for attributing to the President of the United States the powers of a despot; powers which are wholly unknown in any limited monarchy in the world.

The view that he takes as a result of the loose language defining the Executive powers seems exaggerated. But one must agree with him in his condemnation of the view of the Executive power which he says was advanced in Congress. In recent years there has been put forward a similar view by executive officials and to some extent acted on. Men who are not such strict constructionists of the Constitution as Mr. Upshur may well feel real concern if such views are to receive the general acquiescence. Mr. Garfield, when Secretary of the Interior, under Mr. Roosevelt, in his final report to Congress in reference to the power of the Executive over the public domain, said: "Full power under the Constitution was vested in the

Executive Branch of the Government and the extent to which that power may be exercised is governed wholly by the discretion of the Executive unless any specific act has been prohibited either by the Constitution or by legislation."

In pursuance of this principle, Mr. Garfield, under an act for the reclamation of arid land by irrigation, which authorized him to make contracts for irrigation works and incur liability equal to the amount on deposit in the Reclamation Fund, made contracts with associations of settlers by which it was agreed that if these settlers would advance money and work, they might receive certificates from the government engineers of the labor and money furnished by them, and that such certificates might be received in the future in the discharge of their legal obligations to the government for water rent and other things under the statute. It became necessary for the succeeding administration to pass on the validity of these government certificates. They were held by Attorney-General Wickersham to be illegal, on the ground that no authority existed for their issuance. He relied on the Floyd acceptances in 7th Wallace, in which recovery was sought in the Court of Claims on commercial paper in the form of acceptances signed by Mr. Floyd when Secretary of War and delivered to certain contractors. The Court held that they were void because the Secretary of War had no statutory authority to issue them. Mr. Justice Miller, in deciding the case, said:

> The answer which at once suggests itself to one familiar with the structure of our government, in which all power is delegated, and is defined by law, constitutional or statutory, is, that to one or both of these sources we must resort in every instance. We have no officers in this government, from the President down to the most subordinate agent, who does not hold office under the law, with prescribed duties and limited authority. And while some of these, as the President, the Legislature, and the Judiciary, exercise powers in some sense left to the more general definitions necessarily incident to fundamental law found in the Constitution, the larger portion of them are the creation of statutory law, with duties and powers prescribed and limited by that law.

In the light of this view of the Supreme Court it is interesting to compare the language of Mr. Roosevelt in his "Notes for a Possible Autobiography" on the subject of "Executive Powers," in which he says:

The most important factor in getting the right spirit in my Administration, next to insistence upon courage, honesty, and a genuine democracy of desire to serve the plain people, was my insistence upon the theory that the executive power was limited only by specific restrictions and prohibitions appearing in the Constitution or imposed by Congress under its constitutional powers. My view was that every Executive officer and above all every Executive officer in high position was a steward of the people bound actively and affirmatively to do all he could for the people and not to content himself with the negative merit of keeping his talents undamaged in a napkin. I declined to adopt this view that what was imperatively necessary for the Nation could not be done by the President, unless he could find some specific authorization to do it. My belief was that it was not only his right but his duty to do anything that the needs of the Nation demanded unless such action was forbidden by the Constitution or by the laws. Under this interpretation of executive power I did and caused to be done many things not previously done by the President and the heads of the departments. I did not usurp power but I did greatly broaden the use of executive power. In other words, I acted for the common well being of all our people whenever and in whatever measure was necessary, unless prevented by direct constitutional or legislative prohibition.

I may add that Mr. Roosevelt, by way of illustrating his meaning as to the differing usefulness of Presidents, divides the Presidents into two classes, and designates them as "Lincoln Presidents" and "Buchanan Presidents." In order more fully to illustrate his division of Presidents on their merits, he places himself in the Lincoln class of Presidents, and me in the Buchanan class. The identification of Mr. Roosevelt with Mr. Lincoln might otherwise have escaped notice, because there are many differences between the two, presumably superficial, which would give the impartial student of history a different impression. It suggests a story which a friend of mine told of his little daughter Mary. As he came walking home after a business day, she ran out from the house to greet him, all aglow with the importance of what she wished to tell him. She said, "Papa, I am the best scholar in the class." The father's heart throbbed with pleasure as he inquired, "Why, Mary, you surprise me. When did the teacher tell you? This afternoon?" "Oh, no," Mary's reply was, "the teacher didn't tell me—I just noticed it myself."

My judgment is that the view of Mr. Garfield and Mr. Roosevelt, ascribing an undefined residuum of power to the President is an unsafe doctrine and that it might lead under emergencies to results of an arbitrary character, doing irremediable injustice to private right. The mainspring of such a view is that the Executive is charged with responsibility for the welfare of all the people in a general way, that he is to play the part of a Universal Providence and set all things right, and that anything that in his judgment will help the people he ought to do, unless he is expressly forbidden not to do it. The wide field of action that this would give to the Executive one can hardly limit. It is enough to say that Mr. Roosevelt has expressly stated how far he thought this principle would justify him in going in respect to the coal famine and the Pennsylvania anthracite strike which he did so much useful work in settling. What was actually done was the result of his activity, his power to influence public opinion and the effect of the prestige of his great office in bringing the parties to the controversy, the mine owners and the strikers, to a legal settlement by arbitration. No one has a higher admiration for the value of what he did there than I have. But if he had failed in this, he says he intended to take action on his theory of the extent of the executive power already stated. I quote from the same book from which his other words are taken. Mr. Roosevelt says:

> In my own mind, I was already planning effective action, but it was of a very drastic character, and I did not wish to take it until the failure of all other expedients had rendered it necessary. . . . I had definitely determined that somehow or other, act I would, that somehow or other the coal famine should be broken. To accomplish this end it was necessary that the mines should be run, and if I could get no voluntary agreement between the contending sides, that an arbitration commission should be appointed which would command such public confidence as to enable me without too much difficulty, to enforce its terms on the parties. . . .
>
> Meanwhile the Governor of Pennsylvania had all the Pennsylvania militia in the anthracite region although without any effect upon the resumption of mining. The method of action upon which I had determined was to get the Governor of Pennsylvania to ask me to keep order. Then I would put in the army under the command of some first rate general. I would instruct this general to keep absolute order, taking any

steps whatever that were necessary to prevent interference by the strikers or their sympathizers with men who wanted to work. I would also instruct him to dispossess the operators and run the mines as a receiver until such time as the commission might make its report, and until I as President might issue further orders in view of this report.

Now it is perfectly evident that Mr. Roosevelt thinks he was charged with the duty, not only to suppress disorder in Pennsylvania, but to furnish coal to avoid the coal famine in New York and New England, and therefore he proposed to use the army of the United States to mine the coal which should prevent or relieve the famine. It was his avowed intention to take the coal mines out of the hands of their lawful owners and to mine the coal which belonged to them and sell it in the eastern market, against their objection, without any court proceeding of any kind and without any legal obligation on their part to work the mines at all. It was an advocacy of the higher law and his obligation to execute it which is a little startling in a constitutional republic. It is perfectly evident from his statement that it was not the maintenance of law and order in Pennsylvania and the suppression of insurrection, the *only ground* upon which he could intervene at all, that actuated him in what he proposed to do. He used the expression that he would "get" the Governor of Pennsylvania to call for troops from him, and then having secured a formal authority for the use of the army to suppress disorder, he proposed to use it for the seizure of private property and its appropriation for the benefit of the people of other states. The benevolence of his purpose no one can deny, but no one who looks at it from the standpoint of a government of law could regard it as anything but lawless. I venture to think, however, that Mr. Roosevelt is mistaken in what he thinks he would have done. Mr. Roosevelt in office was properly amenable to the earnest advice of those whom he trusted, and there were men about him who would probably have dissuaded him from such a course.

I am aware that there are many who believe in government ownership of the sources of public comfort in the interest of the community at large; but it is certainly only the extremes of that school that favor the use of the army under the President to seize the needed mines without constitutional amendment or legislative and judicial action and without compensation. Mr. Roosevelt in his subsequent remarks seems to find a justification for his general view of the limitations of Executive power in what Mr. Lincoln did during the Civil War. That Mr. Lincoln with the stress of the greatest civil war in modern times felt called upon to do things, the constitutionality of which was seriously questioned, is undoubtedly true. But Mr. Lincoln always pointed out the source of the authority which in his opinion justified his acts, and there was always a strong ground for maintaining the view which he took. His claim of right to suspend the writ of *habeas corpus* I venture to think was well founded. Congress subsequently expressly gave him this right and the Supreme Court sustained his exercise of it under the act of Congress. His Emancipation Proclamation was attacked as an unconstitutional exercise of authority, but he defended it as an act of the Commander-in-Chief justified by military necessity to weaken the enemies of the Nation and suppress their rebellion. Certainly the arguments that he and those who supported his action brought to sustain it have great weight. But Mr. Lincoln never claimed that whatever authority in government was not expressly denied to him he could exercise.

In my reading recently I ran across a case which attracted great attention at the time, now more than one hundred years ago. It concerned the action of another President of great popularity, great power, great mental activity, and great and equally genuine sympathy with the people and with popular government—Thomas Jefferson. Mr. Jefferson was a strict constructionist of the Constitution in theory and in practice, but as in the case of all of us, when he had power things looked differently to him and acts were justified in his mind and conscience on the theory that he was doing good and working for the public welfare. But in his wide view of what he himself as President could do to preserve the public welfare, he did something that troubled him, even after he left the Presidency.

The owner of a large tract of land reaching to the Mississippi River, just outside of New Orleans, and a part of its suburbs, claimed title to an alluvial extension of that land deposited by the river, as lawful accretion to his property. Such an accretion was known in French legal nomenclature as a "Batture." The owner sought by suit in the Territorial Court to exclude from the Batture people of the city who took sand therefrom. The Territorial Court sustained the title of the riparian owner to the Batture. In this litigation Edward Livingston, who had gone from New York to New Orleans, just after the acquisition of the Territory, appeared as counsel for the owner and as part of his compensation received some of the land. He attempted to improve it, to protect it against the wearing of the river and to build a canal through it. The territorial governor was Claiborn, and the people of the town who had been shut out by the action of the local court appealed to him. He submitted the matter to Mr. Jefferson, who consulted his Attorney-General, Mr. Rodney, and thereupon issued a warrant directing the United States Marshal to take possession of the land in question and hold it for the benefit of the people of New Orleans, under a Statute of Congress authorizing the President to exclude squatters from the public domain. The local court issued an injunction against the marshal's complying with this order of the President. The marshal refused to obey the injunction, and using Federal troops opened the land to the use of the people of the city, who continued to take sand. This exposed the land to the danger which it was being improved to prevent. The river rose and swept away the works. Livingston lost a very large sum of money by reason of this invasion. He went to Washington twice, to be heard, and was refused an opportunity to argue the case, or to know the grounds upon which action of the President had been taken, or to see the opinion of the Attorney-General upon which it was based. He petitioned Congress for relief without avail. Finally he brought suit against Jefferson personally for trespass in the Federal Court of Virginia. The suit was dismissed by Chief Justice Marshall of the Federal Court on the ground that the court in Virginia had no jurisdiction of a trespass committed on land in Louisiana.

Thereafter Mr. Jefferson published a defense of his action which brought out an answer from Livingston, which was so convincing on the issues made by Mr. Jefferson and was so replete with wit and humor and satire that even the British Encyclopedia describes it as crushing. In the course of this answer Livingston used some language that it seems to me would have been properly applicable to the proceeding which Mr. Roosevelt proposed to take, and which he frankly calls drastic. Mr. Roosevelt says there would doubtless have been an outcry against his proceeding. It would have been denounced as a usurpation; but he thinks that the good he would have done would have rallied to his support the great body of the people in whose interest he would have acted and thus his plan would have vindicated itself. Mr. Livingston opened his answer to Jefferson as follows:

When a public functionary abuses his power by an act which bears on the community, his conduct excites attention, provokes popular resentment, and seldom fails to receive the punishment it merits. Should an individual be chosen for the victim, little sympathy is created for his sufferings, if the interest of all is supposed to be promoted by the ruin of one. The gloss of zeal for the public is therefore always spread over acts of oppression, and as a brilliant exertion of energy in their favor, which, when viewed in its true light, would be found a fatal blow to their rights.

In no government is this effect so easily produced as in a free republic; party spirit, inseparable from its existence, there aids the illusion, and a popular leader is allowed in many instances impunity, and sometimes rewarded with applause for acts that would make a tyrant tremble on his throne. This evil must exist in a degree—it is founded in the natural course of human passions; but in a wise and enlightened nation it will be restrained; and the consciousness that it must exist will make such a people more watchful to prevent its abuse. These reflections occur to one, whose property, without trial or any of the forms of law, has been violently seized by the first magistrate of the Union,—who has hitherto vainly solicited an inquiry into his title,—who has seen the conduct of his oppressor excused or applauded,—and who, in the book he is now about to examine, finds an attempt openly to justify that conduct upon principles as dangerous as the act was illegal and unjust.

Mr. Livingston ended his answer to Mr. Jefferson as follows:

My future conduct will depend much on that of my adversary. I shall continue to reply to every argument that may be addressed to the public on this subject. Knowing that my cause is good, I do not despair, even with humble pretensions, to make its justice appear. For this purpose, I have always courted investigation: I should have preferred it in a court of justice, but do not decline it before the public.

Though some may condemn me only on hearing the name of my opponent, there are many, very many, in the nation who have independence enough to judge for themselves, and the ability to decide with correctness; to such I submit the merits of a controversy which has been rendered interesting as well from the constitutional as the legal questions it involves, and on which Mr. Jefferson has, by his management of it, staked his legal, his political, and almost his moral reputation. That he should not have understood the nature of my title and the different foreign codes on which it depends, is no reproach; that he should have acted at all without this knowledge must surprise, that he should have acted forcibly, must astonish us; but that he should persevere in the same pretence of understanding the law of France better than gentlemen bred to it from their childhood, and who, engaged in the same side of the controversy with himself, have abandoned the ground he has taken— that he should obstinately justify an invasion of private property, in a manner that puts it in the power of a President with impunity to commit acts of oppression at which a King would tremble—that he should do all this, and still talk of conscious rectitude, must amaze all those who look only to the reputation he has enjoyed, and who do not consider the inconsistency of human nature, and the deplorable effects of an inordinate passion for popularity.

The life of Edward Livingston is one of the most romantic and checkered that I know. He was a brother of Chancellor Livingston, and a son of an earlier Judge Livingston. He was born in the Colony of New York, and was given a thorough education in languages and in both the common and the civil law. He was a gifted speaker and had a style both pleasant and trenchant, which he illuminated with wit, humor and satire and with the most graceful literary references. He was a very earnest Republican and a follower of Jefferson. He was elected to Congress as a Republican in the days of the first Adams, and introduced the resolutions, already noted, denouncing Adams as a usurper of individual right in granting the extradition of the British murderer who was arrested in South Carolina. These resolutions were the occasion for the wonderful argument of John Marshall, also a member of Congress, to which I have referred. After Mr. Livingston had served in Congress for two terms, he was appointed by Mr. Jefferson to be United States District Attorney for New York. He was also at the same time (for they allowed plurality of offices in those days), appointed to be Mayor of New York by Governor Clinton. Mr. Livingston was a free liver and most hospitable. The yellow fever came to New York. As Mayor, Mr. Livingston was active in dealing with the epidemic and endeared himself to the people by his efforts to save them. During the epidemic, an agent of the government visited New York, examined Mr. Livingston's accounts and found that in his collections for the government he was short a large sum. It at first was thought to be one hundred thousand dollars, but was subsequently found to be not more than forty thousand. It turned out that a good deal of this was due to the dishonesty of a subordinate, but Livingston could not relieve himself entirely from the charge of defalcation which was probably due to his lack of care in his accounts. When the matter was brought to his attention, he resigned both offices, turned all his property over to the government, and left for New Orleans, a territory which in the year before, in 1803, had been taken over by the United States under a treaty negotiated by his brother, Chancellor Robert Livingston. By his defalcation he passed out of the good graces of Mr. Jefferson, and Mr. Jefferson's attitude in respect to the litigation in which Mr. Livingston took part is possibly explained by his irritation at the disgrace which he felt that Livingston had put upon his administration. Though ruined by the action of Mr. Jefferson in respect to the Batture, Mr. Livingston continued the practice of the law and paid the Government in full. He was in New Orleans at the time of the famous battle fought there by Old Hickory. General Jackson came to know Mr. Livingston and to value him highly, and used him for legal advice before and after the battle. Mr. Livingston appeared for General Jackson in responding to a summons issued by Judge Hall for contempt on the part of the General in ignoring a writ of *habeas corpus* which he had issued, and in otherwise treating the Judge contemptuously. After the battle, General Jackson recognized the jurisdiction of the court, and submitted to its authority, upon Mr. Livingston's advice. The friendship made with General Jackson, Mr. Livingston continued to enjoy during his life. He subsequently became a member of Congress from Louisiana, a United States Senator from the state, and was finally appointed Secretary of State under General Jackson. Mr. Livingston wrote a code of procedure for the Territory of Louisiana to reconcile the civil law practice to the anomalies which the adoption of the state into a Union with so many common law jurisdictions presented. This code was adopted. The great reputation which Mr. Livingston obtained, however, was from a criminal code which he wrote for the state of Louisiana, but which that state did not adopt. In its humanity and its provisions for prison reform, it was fifty years ahead of his time.

I venture to say that no American jurist among the jurists of continental Europe made a deeper impression than did Mr. Livingston by his Criminal Code. It is of the utmost interest to note the fact that after he had published his code and had received from it the highest commendations from Chief Justice Marshall, Chancellor Kent and Mr. Justice Story, and all the great jurists of the country, Mr. Jefferson wrote him a letter congratulating him upon it and assuring him of his respect and friendship. After Mr. Jefferson's death, Mr. Livingston was arguing a case in the Supreme Court of the United States when the other side quoted from his answer to Jefferson as to the Batture. In the course of his argument he referred to the answer and said that it was written under a sense of having a great wrong done him by Mr. Jefferson, and that he had not changed his view since writing it. But he said he thought he owed it to the memory of Mr. Jefferson to say that in after years Mr. Jefferson renewed his friendly relations with him, and showed by his conduct the greatness which a French writer recognizes in a man who having done an injury to another is able to forgive that other.

Recurring now to the plan of Mr. Roosevelt as to the coal mines of Pennsylvania, I think that if we substitute for the individual Livingston, in the Batture controversy, the anthracite mine owners, the language of Mr. Livingston which I have quoted would be germane in such a discussion. I would not dwell upon this subject were it not of great importance with reference to the course urged upon President Wilson when he had sent Federal troops for the maintenance of order in Colorado. He was advised to use the troops to close the mines which were then running and producing a substantial part of their normal product. The closing of mines might have been a sop to those who threatened violence in case the troops were withdrawn and so mitigate lawlessness for a time. But was it a proper method of maintaining order to deprive men of the right of property that it was the very object of the constitutional provision for Federal intervention to protect? No one claimed the operation of the mines was unlawful. It was only said that their continued operation after the withdrawal of the Federal troops would lead to disturbance. By whom? By the strikers. Was this not a proposition to compel an owner of property to cease its lawful use because his former employees would otherwise attempt unlawfully and violently to prevent such use?

I have now concluded a review of the Executive power, and hope that I have shown that it is limited, so far as it is possible to limit such a power consistent with that discretion and promptness of action that are essential to preserve the interests of the public in times of emergency, or legislative neglect or inaction.

There is little danger to the public weal from the tyranny or reckless character of a President who is not sustained by the people. The absence of popular support will certainly in the course of two years withdraw from him the sympathetic action of at least one House of Congress, and by the control that that House has over appropriations, the Executive arm can be paralyzed, unless he resorts to a coup d'état, which means impeachment, conviction and deposition. The only danger in the action of the Executive under the present limitations and lack of limitation of his powers is when his popularity is such that he can be sure of the support of the electorate and therefore of Congress, and when the majority in the legislative halls respond with alacrity and sycophancy to his will. This condition cannot probably be long continued. We have had Presidents who felt the public pulse with accuracy, who played their parts upon the political stage with histrionic genius and commanded the people almost as if they were an army and the President their Commander-in-Chief. Yet in all these cases, the good sense of the people has ultimately prevailed and no danger has been done to our political structure and the reign of law has continued. In such times when the Executive power seems to be all prevailing, there have always been men in this free and intelligent people of ours, who apparently courting political humiliation and disaster have registered protest against this undue Executive domination and this use of the Executive power and popular support to perpetuate itself.

The cry of Executive domination is often entirely unjustified, as when the President's commanding influence only grows out of a proper cohesion of a party and its recognition of the necessity for political leadership; but the fact that Executive domination is regarded as a useful ground for attack upon a successful administration, even when there is no ground for it, is itself proof of the dependence we may properly place upon the sanity and clear perceptions of the people in avoiding its baneful effects when there is real danger. Even if a vicious precedent is set by the Executive, and injustice done, it does not have the same bad effect that an improper precedent of a court may have, for one President does not consider himself bound by the policies or constitutional views of his predecessors.

The Constitution does give the President wide discretion and great power, and it ought to do so. It calls from him activity and energy to see that within his proper sphere he does what his great responsibilities and opportunities require. He is no figurehead, and it is entirely proper that an energetic and active clear-sighted people, who, when they have work to do, wish it done well, should be willing to rely upon their judgment in selecting their Chief Agent, and having selected him, should entrust to him all the power needed to carry out their governmental purpose, great as it may be.

THE UNITED STATES
AND PEACE

The United States and Peace

Commentary

Frank X. Gerrity

William Howard Taft's concern with issues of foreign policy dated back to his years as governor of the Philippines and inevitably broadened in his service as secretary of war and president of the United States. There is a certain element of irony in the fact that his formal writings on foreign affairs are concentrated in his post-presidential years, when he held no public office but, as a private citizen, taught law at Yale University.

The books in question, *The United States and Peace* (1914) and *Taft Papers on League of Nations* (1920), range over a variety of topics, from the nature and limits of the Monroe Doctrine, through the protection of the treaty rights of aliens resident in the United States, to the overarching theme of effective international organization for settlement of disputes and preservation of the peace.

The earlier of these works by Taft, *The United States and*

Peace, a collection of four lectures sponsored by the New York Peace Society and delivered in the winter of 1913–14, just before the outbreak of the European war, provides an excellent example of Taft's lawyerly and scholarly approach to foreign policy analysis. Three of the talks touch on topics that had stirred controversy in the Taft administration and that continued to lend a certain acidity to Taft's comments on the words and actions of his electoral adversaries of 1912. The fourth was a more scholarly exercise, an historical exploration of peacekeeping federations over the centuries that was prompted by the interest of Hamilton Holt, editor of *The Independent,* where the lectures were first published.

Taft's view of the Monroe Doctrine was positive; he saw it as a national asset, a policy that had generally worked to safeguard the United States and its American neighbors against European intrusions. He was not concerned, as other peace advocates tended to be, that the Monroe Doctrine's efficacy rested ultimately on force, the power of the American army and navy to ensure respect. Taft was even less in sympathy with those who saw the Monroe Doctrine as an antiquated "shibboleth" that promoted friction with our Latin neighbors, asserted a "suzerainty" over our neighboring states, kept developed states like Argentina, Brazil, and Chile (the ABC countries) on leading strings, and engendered resentments that interfered with our trade with Latin America.

Taft emphasized what he described as the "limitations" of the Monroe Doctrine. First of all, it was a U.S. policy, not international law binding on any other country, target, or beneficiary. Secondly, it was invoked only in the interest of the "peace and safety" of the United States. A principle of propinquity also operated—the closer an area was to the

United States, the greater the American interest. (The Caribbean and Central American areas provided a prime example. There Taft, as president, had practiced "Dollar Diplomacy"—using financial clout more than military muscle—in his effort to protect the approaches to the new Panama Canal.) Furthermore, the ABC powers were not only at a stage of development at which American protection was unnecessary, but also so distant from the United States that it was unlikely that American security interests would ever become involved there. Taft agreed that the cultural sensitivities of the Latin republics should be respected, but he thought it improbable that the American republics would unite to multilateralize the Monroe Doctrine. He certainly overestimated the success of his Latin American policy, and "Dollar Diplomacy" proved to be more a palliative than a cure for American problems with the republics to the south. But was his policy less successful than those of the administrations that preceded and followed his?

For the maintenance of peace in an increasingly democratic world, Taft asserted in his second lecture, it is important that each stable government be able to perform its promises to other nations promptly and effectively. An especial concern of his was the danger that the United States might become involved in war because of the inability of the federal government to enforce the treaty rights of aliens resident in the United States.

Taft detailed major incidents of mob violence against foreigners, from 1811 to 1910, in which victims, conspicuously Asians, Mexicans, and Italians, had been treated atrociously—killed, grievously wounded, or evicted. Congress had made indemnity payments to the victims or their families, but Taft could find no instance in which perpetrators of these attacks had been punished. Local authorities either in sympathy with or cowed by hostile public sentiment had failed to carry out, even in cases of homicide, effective investigations leading to punishment. This, said Taft, "is not a record in which we can take pride."

Some of these episodes seriously strained relations with the victims' home governments, but the State Department's routine defense invoked the federal system and its assignment of general law-enforcement authority to state governments. The standard treaty of that era provided that resident aliens have the ordinary protections of the law available to citizens of the host country. The State Department argued that such treaty obligations were satisfied, since American citizens, as well as resident aliens, fell under the jurisdiction of the state courts.

To a jurist this was an unsatisfactory defense; to a statesman concerned with averting occasions for war it constituted a major miscalculation. Taft's predecessors in the presidential office, Harrison, McKinley, and Roosevelt, had each offered the obvious solution—Congressional legislation extending the law-enforcement authority of the federal government to include the protection of the rights of resident aliens. Taft endorsed their approach but was no more successful than they in winning its enactment.

In this lecture, he reviewed the general arguments in support of an extension of federal authority to deal with local behavior that might involve the whole country in war. He cited regional variations in the quality of law enforcement, the susceptibility of local officials to community pressure—a susceptibility intensified by the introduction of mechanisms for the recall of officials, even judges!—the superior resources of federal investigators and prosecutors, and so forth. But he reserved his most withering fire for a report of a committee of the American Bar Association from 1892, on which, he believed, the consistent Congressional opposition had been based. Taft found the committee report (which was never adopted by the American Bar Association) rife with factual, juridical, and logical error. He rejected its strict constructionist doubts on the constitutionality of such expansive legislation. He pointed out that in *Baldwin v. Franks* (1887) the Supreme Court of the United States, in a decision ignored by the committee, had clearly found that the federal government has the power to enact legislation to protect the treaty rights of aliens, although no such statutes had ever been enacted. Taft, however, saw no need to rely solely on the treaty power or the identification of treaties as part of the "supreme law of the land" but went beyond that to argue that the general grant of legislative authority, the "necessary and proper" clause, gave Congress all the requisite authority. His contention was strengthened by the weight of general acceptance in the decades that followed.

In his third lecture, President Taft turned to a topic in which he had long had an interest: the maintenance of peace through the promotion of international arbitration. He acknowledged that not all contentions were susceptible to resolution by arbitration and, therefore, that such treaties would not always provide a practical means of settlement, but he nonetheless saw such treaties as a useful instrument of American policy.

His specific concern was, however, the Senate's persistent opposition to general treaties of arbitration. In the wake of the Venezuela Boundary Dispute (1895), Richard Olney, Grover Cleveland's secretary of state, had negotiated a bilateral treaty of arbitration with Great Britain to facilitate peaceful settlement of any future disputes between the two governments. The Olney-Pauncefote Treaty as proposed was, however, rejected by the Senate. The Senate's insistence on the right to give "advice and consent" on the terms not only of the general arbitration treaty but also of each specific arbitration brought forward under the general treaty rendered general treaties of arbitration meaningless. Proposals for general agreements of arbitration or conciliation advanced by subsequent administrations, including Taft's, would all fall before this same constitutional impediment.

The prospects for international arrangements for the settlement of disputes were favorable, as the enthusiasm for the Hague Conferences attests, and efforts to overcome the senatorial obstacle taxed the ingenuity of highly competent officials in the State Department and the White House. John Hay, Roosevelt's first secretary of state, negotiated general treaties of arbitration with (Taft thought) rather loosely defined areas of jurisdiction—"all questions of a legal nature"—excluding matters of national honor or vital interest. Such issues would be submitted to the Hague Tribunal for adjudication. If differences with respect to jurisdiction or procedure arose between the parties involved, a "specific agreement" of submission would be entered into. When the Senate substituted "treaty" for "specific agreement" prior to approving the treaties, Roosevelt declined to proceed with ratification, noting that such treaties brought the United States no closer to arbitration than it had been in the absence of a treaty. The Senate's rejoinder: Approval of the treaty as submitted would constitute an unlawful delegation of the Senate's treaty-making power to the president.

Hay's successor as secretary of state, Elihu Root, a shrewd Wall Street lawyer, negotiated twenty-five arbitration treaties, each of which excluded almost all matters of substantive importance and included a provision for a second treaty subject to Senate approval. Root succeeded in gaining the consent of the Senate, and the treaties went into effect. They proved to be as meaningless as Theodore Roosevelt had predicted they would be.

Taft and his secretary of state, Philander C. Knox, in treaties negotiated with Great Britain and France in 1911, put forward an ingenious new model combining a reasonably well defined area of jurisdiction with respect for the claims of the Senate. It limited arbitration to "justiciable" matters, that is, matters susceptible to resolution by application of the principles of law or equity. A Joint High Commission had authority to decide which matters were "justiciable" and to render advisory reports on nonjusticiable questions. In each instance of arbitration, a second treaty would define the powers of the arbitrator, the points at issue, and other relevant conditions. The Senate was not satisfied. The independent functions of the High Commission provoked a flurry of amendments before the Senate approved mutilated versions of the treaties by overwhelming votes. An embarrassed Taft, to use his own words, "put them on the shelf and let the dust accumulate on them."

Former president Taft effectively argued the merits of arbitration, particularly *vis a vis* France and Great Britain, cited American precedents, and offered a devastating critique of the contention, central to the Senate's argument, that permitting arbitration tribunals to make judgments on issues previously defined by treaty constitutes an improper delegation of the Senate's treaty-making powers. In doing so, he mounted a strong retrospective defense of the Taft-Knox treaties.

The final lecture links the "federative trend in international affairs" to the movement toward universal peace. Taft's historical survey of federative polities sweeps across the centuries, from the Achaean League of classical Greece to the dominions of the British Empire in the early twentieth century. While federations of states were commonly motivated by the need to marshal resources to defend against an outside threat, implicit in a federation was some arrangement to resolve disputes within or between member states. Taft's story of the very gradual development of the concept of an independent judiciary is equally sweeping: from Old Testament "judges," through Greek assemblies and Roman praetors, to feudal and royal courts, and finally, in good whiggish fashion, to Anglo-American jurisprudence with judges as independent officers whose responsibility it was to decide disputes impartially on the basis of the law and the facts. Taft held that this Anglo-American concept of an independent judiciary should find an important place in international relations. Unfortunately, he argued, the permanent court of arbitration established at the First Hague Conference, with its long list of potential arbitrators and elective participation, did not fill this need.

The Second Conference's proposal for a permanent prize court, with its cadre of judges appointed by the major nations and supplemented by other judges assigned from a rota, was more relevant. Rulings from national prize courts could be appealed to the international tribunal, and its decisions were to be binding on all parties. Although an implementing document, the Declaration of London, was not accepted by Great Britain, the major maritime power, the structure of the international prize court provided the framework for a permanent international court of justice with paid members whose role would be limited to service as judges in international disputes. Taft saw this style of arbitration as vastly superior to the traditional mixed commission, with its constant temptation to decide on political rather than judicial grounds—to split the difference—which discouraged the government with the stronger case from submitting to arbitration. Taft was optimistic that such a permanent tribunal would build a body of case law that would encourage nations to submit more and more cases to its adjudication. He anticipated that within fifty or so years the great powers would have adhered to a convention requiring that all justiciable disputes be submitted to this permanent tribunal.

In many ways Taft shared the optimism engendered by his era's confidence in the idea of progress, an optimism tempered in Taft by lawyerly prudence. Revolutions in communication and transportation had advanced understanding among the nations of the world, a great missionary effort and the work of universities had elevated moral standards, the advantages of peace had become so obvious that there would be universal willingness to submit international disputes to arbitration, and international public opinion would assure the acceptance of the tribunal's decisions. On the eve of the outbreak of war in Europe, ex-president Taft could envision a Tennysonian "Parliament of Man, the Federation of the world."

Foreword

Every President of the United States can be quoted in favor of peace. From the first great Virginian to the last all have abhorred what Thomas Jefferson called "the greatest scourge of mankind."

No President, however, has espoused the cause more unreservedly, has grasped its fundamental principles more thoroughly or attempted to advance its progress more directly than has Mr. Taft. This book is a demonstration of the fact.

Mr. Taft has occupied the greatest political office in the world. He has presided over a confederation of nearly half a hundred sovereign States—the greatest peace society known to history and a living example to the nations of the earth of the way to obtain peace through political organization. Peace is the outcome of justice, justice of law, law of political organization. Emanuel Kant proclaimed this as the true philosophy of peace, when in 1795 he wrote: "We never can have universal peace until the world is politically organized, and it will never be possible to organize the world politically until the people, not the kings, rule."

Peace hath her victories no less renowned than war. Perhaps the greatest victory yet achieved is the declaration of Mr. Taft, as President of the United States, that he was willing to refer all questions, even those involving national honor, to arbitration. He attempted to negotiate treaties to this end with Great Britain and France. His hope was that the example thus afforded would be followed by other nations, until a general treaty could be formulated in which the peoples of the earth would agree to refer all their disputes to a court of arbitral justice. This would be the doom of war.

The attempt, though thwarted by the United States Senate, offers the nations a guiding principle which they will support with an ever-increasing favor and fervor until it is made a universal law. Mr. Taft's high statesmanship has inaugurated a movement that will not end until, as Victor Hugo prophesied, "the only battle-field will be the market opening to commerce and the mind opening to new ideas."

The present volume is the outcome of a suggestion made to Mr. Taft by the New York Peace Society, which has started so many good movements to further international progress and comity. Its four chapters were delivered last winter as lectures under the auspices of the Society. They were also published as contributions to *The Independent.* A special importance attaches to them in the fact that they were prepared by one who has been a supreme and responsible leader in national and international politics. Thus the age-long dreams of the poets, prophets and philosophers have at last entered the realm of practical statesmanship.

The first chapter deals with the Monroe Doctrine. This constitutes altogether the most important foreign policy of the United States. The second chapter discusses the status of aliens under the conflicting jurisdiction of the Federal and State Governments. This involves our chief danger of war. The third chapter completely refutes the claim of the Senate that it has no power to consent to general arbitration treaties. This, if persisted in, will block all further participation of the United States in the movement for extending the scope of arbitration. The fourth chapter elucidates the history and conception of a world federation in which is emphasized a court of judicial arbitration with jurisdiction of all disputes—"the highest court of appeals this side the bar of Eternal Justice." Its realization is only a matter of decades.

The one way for a man to rise above the presidency of the United States is to ascend into the international realm and there work for peace through justice. Mr. Taft has taken this upward step. This book is a Declaration of Interdependence.

Hamilton Holt

1

The Monroe Doctrine

Its Limitations and Implications

It is now ninety years since what the world has always called the Monroe Doctrine was announced by President Monroe in a message to Congress. It was a declaration to the world that any effort on the part of an European government to force its political system upon a people of this hemisphere, or to oppress it, would affect the safety of the United States and would be inimical to her interests, and, further, that the subjecting to colonization by any European government of any part of the two American continents, all of which was held to be within the lawful jurisdiction of some government, would be equally objectionable. The first part of the declaration was prompted by the fear that the then Holy Alliance of Russia, Prussia, Austria, and France would attempt to assist Spain in reconquering the Central and South American republics that had revolted from Spain and set up independent governments which had been recognized by the United States. The other part, against colonization, was prompted by certain claims that Russia was making to take control over territory on the northwest coast of North America to which the United States then asserted title. There was expressly excepted from the doctrine thus announced any purpose to interfere with Spain's effort to regain her lost colonies or the continued exercise of jurisdiction by European governments over any colonies or territories which they then had in America.

I have not space to give the details of the instances in which our Presidents, representing our country in its foreign relations, found it necessary to insist upon compliance with the Monroe Doctrine. When Mr. Webster was secretary of state, he declined, in Mr. Tyler's name, to consider a proposition by England and France for a joint agreement with Spain as to the disposition of Cuba, stating that, while the United States did not intend to interfere with the control of Cuba by Spain, it could not consent to the ownership of the island by any other power. Again, when Yucatan had been temporarily separated from Mexico by insurrection, and the insurrection leaders sought to dispose of the country to us, or to England, or to Spain, President Polk, in declining their offer to the United States, advised them that we could not consent to a transfer of dominion and sovereignty either to Spain, Great Britain, or any other power, because it would be "dangerous to our peace and safety."

Without directly citing the Monroe Doctrine by name, Mr. Seward protested against the occupation of Mexico by France during the Civil War with the purpose of colonizing or setting up a new government on the ruins of the Mexican Government. France denied having any other purpose than to collect its debts and redress its wrongs. Afterward the Mexican Government was overthrown and an empire established with an Austrian archduke at its head. The American Civil War closed, the American troops were massed on the Mexican border under Sheridan, and France was requested to withdraw her troops. She did so, and the collapse of the Maximilian government followed.

President Grant, in sending the Santo Domingo treaty to the Senate, announced that thereafter no territory on the continent should be regarded as subject to transfer to an European power, and that this was an adherence to the Monroe Doctrine as a measure of national protection.

Again, the policy was insisted upon and maintained by Mr. Olney and Mr. Cleveland in reference to England's declination to arbitrate the boundary issue between Venezuela and British Guyana, in which Mr. Cleveland and Mr. Olney believed that they saw a desire on the part of Great Britain, through a boundary dispute, to sequester a considerable part of Venezuela, valuable because of the discovery of gold-mines in it. Mr. Cleveland's position in the matter was sustained by a resolution which was passed by both houses. In this instance Mr. Olney used the expression: "Today the United States is practically sovereign on this continent, and its fiat is law upon the subjects to which it confines its interposition."

The original declaration of the Monroe Doctrine was prompted by England's wish, when Canning was foreign minister, that England and the United States should make a joint declaration of such a policy. Since its announcement by President Monroe there have been frequent intimations by English statesmen while in office that they do not object to its maintenance. Whether the other governments of Europe have acquiesced in it or not, it is certain that none of them have insisted upon violating it when the matter was called to their attention by the United States. Every one admits that its maintenance until recently has made for the peace of the world, has kept European governments from intermeddling in the politics of this hemisphere, and has enabled all the various Latin-American republics that were offshoots from Spain to maintain their own governments and their independence. While it may be truly said that it has not made for peace between them, still, that was not within the scope of its purpose. It has, however, restrained the land-hunger and the growing disposition for colonization by some European governments which otherwise would certainly have carried them into this hemisphere. The very revolutions and instabilities of many of the Latin-American republics would have offered frequent excuse and opportunity for intervention by European governments which they would have promptly improved.

But now we are told that under changed conditions the Monroe Doctrine has become an obsolete shibboleth, that it promotes friction with our Latin-American neighbors, and that it is time for us to abandon it. It is said that it is an assertion of a suzerainty by the United States over both continents; that it seeks to keep under the tutelage of the United States great and powerful nations like the Argentine Republic, Brazil, and Chile; that its continuance as a declared policy of this government alienates these and other republics of South America, injures their proper national pride, creates a resentment against us which interferes with our trade relations, and does not promote the friendly feeling that strengthens the cause of peace.

Before we proceed to consider this proposition we ought to make clear certain definite limitations of the Monroe policy that are not always given weight by those who condemn it. In the first place, the Monroe Doctrine is a policy of the United States and is not an obligation of international law binding upon any of the countries affected, either the European countries whose action it seeks to limit or the countries whose government and territory it seeks to protect. Nor, indeed, does it create an absolute obligation on the part of the United States to enforce it. It rests primarily upon the danger to the interest and safety of the United States, and, therefore, the nearer to her boundaries the attempted violation of the doctrine, the more directly her safety is affected and the more acute her interest, and, naturally, therefore, the more extreme will be the measures to which she would resort to enforce it. While the assertion of the doctrine covers both continents, the measures of the United States in objecting to an invasion of the policy might be much less emphatic in the case where it was attempted in countries as remote as Argentina, Brazil, and Chile than in the countries surrounding the Caribbean Sea, or brought close to the United States by the opening of the Panama Canal. It is well that the declared policy has in the past covered both continents, because this certainly contributed to the causes which made Argentina, Brazil, and Chile the powerful countries they have become. But, as Daniel Webster said in Congress in 1826, speaking of the plans of the Holy Alliance:

> If an armament had been furnished by the allies to act against provinces the most remote from us, as Chile or Buenos Ayres, the distance of the scene of action diminishing our apprehension of danger, and diminishing also our means of effectual interposition, might still have left us to content ourselves with remonstrance. But a very different case would have arisen if an army equipped and maintained by these powers had been landed on the shores of the Gulf of Mexico and commenced the war in our own immediate neighborhood. Such an event might justly be regarded as dangerous to ourselves, and on that ground call for decided and immediate interference by us.

In other words, the extent of our intervention to enforce the policy is a matter of our own judgment, with a notice that it may cover all America. It therefore follows that the Monroe Doctrine, so far as it applies to Argentina, Brazil, and Chile, the so-called A B C governments of South America, is now never likely to be pressed, first because they have reached such a point that they are able to protect themselves against any European interference, and, second, because they are so remote from us that a violation of the doctrine with respect to them would be little harmful to our interests and safety.

The second great limitation of the Monroe Doctrine is that it does not contemplate any interference on our part with the right of an European government to declare and make war upon any American government, or to pursue such course in the vindication of its national rights as would be a proper method under the rules of international law. This was expressly declared to be a proper term in the statement of the Doctrine by Mr. Seward during our Civil War, when Spain made war against Chile. He announced our intention to observe neutrality between the two nations, and he laid down the proposition that the Doctrine did not require the United States, in a consistent pursuit of it, to protect any government in this hemisphere, either by a defensive alliance against the attacking European power or by interfering to prevent such punishment as it might inflict, provided only that in the end the conquering power did not force its own government upon the conquered people, or compel a permanent transfer to it of their territory, or resort to any other unjustly oppressive measures against them. And Mr. Roosevelt, in his communications to Congress, has again and again asserted that maintenance of the Doctrine does not require our government to object to armed measures on the part of European governments to collect their debts and the debts of their nationals against governments in this continent that are in default of their just obligations, provided only that they do not attempt to satisfy those obligations by taking over to themselves ownership and possession of the territory of the debtor governments or by other oppressive measures. It may be conceded that Mr. Olney used language that was unfortunate in describing the effect of the Monroe Doctrine upon the position of the United States in this hemisphere. It is not remarkable that it has been construed to be the claim of suzerainty over the territory of the two American continents. Our fiat is not law to control the domestic concerns or, indeed, the foreign policies of the Latin-American republics or of other American governments, nor do we exercise substantial sovereignty over them. We are concerned that their governments shall not be interfered with by European governments;

we are concerned that this hemisphere shall not be a field for land aggrandizement and the chase for increased political power by European governments, such as we have witnessed in Africa and in China and Manchuria, and we believe that such a condition would be inimical to our safety and interests. More than this, where a controversy between an European government and a Latin-American republic is of such a character that it is likely to lead to war, we feel that our earnest desire to escape the possible result against which the Monroe Doctrine is aimed is sufficient to justify our mediating between the European power and the Latin-American republic, and bringing about by negotiation, if possible, a peaceable settlement of the difference. This is what Mr. Roosevelt did in Venezuela and in Santo Domingo. It was not that the use of force or threatened force to collect their debts by the European powers constituted a violation of the Monroe Doctrine that induced Mr. Roosevelt to act, but only a general desire to promote peace and also a wish to avoid circumstances in which an invasion of the Monroe Doctrine might easily follow.

It is said—and this is what frightens peace advocates from the Monroe Doctrine—that it rests on force and ultimately on the strength of our army and our navy. That is true, if its enforcement is resisted. Its ultimate sanction and vindication are in our ability to maintain it; but our constant upholding and assertion of the Doctrine have enabled us, with the conflicting interests of European powers—the support of some and the acquiescence of others—to give effect to the Doctrine for now nearly a century, and that without the firing of a single shot. This has secured the Doctrine a traditional weight that assertion of a new policy by the United States never could have. It is a national asset, and, indeed, an asset of the highest value for those who would promote the peace of the world. The mere fact that the further successful maintenance of the Monroe Doctrine, in the improbable event that any European power shall deliberately violate it, will require the exercise of force upon our part is certainly not a reason for the most sincere advocate of peace to insist upon sacrificing its beneficent influence and prestige as an instrument of peace to prevent European intermeddling in this hemisphere which a century of successful insistence without actual use of force has given it.

Much as the Doctrine may be criticised by the Continental press of Europe, it is an institution of one hundred years' standing; it is something that its age is bound to make Europe respect. It was advanced at a time when we were but a small nation with little power, and it has acquired additional force and prestige as we have grown to our present size and strength and international influence.

Were we to abandon the Doctrine and thus, in effect, notify the European governments that, so far as our remonstrance or interposition was concerned, they might take possession of Santo Domingo, of Haiti, or of any of the Central American republics, or of any South American republics that might be disturbed by revolution and that might give them some international excuse for intervention, it would be but a very short time before we would be forced into controversies that would be much more dangerous to the peace of this hemisphere than our continued assertion of the Doctrine properly understood and limited.

I fully sympathize with the desire to make such countries as the Argentine Republic, Brazil, Chile, and other powers in South America that are acquiring stability and maintaining law and order within their boundaries, understand that we do not claim to exercise over them any suzerainty at all and that we are not tendering our guardianship as if they were children or as if they needed it. We reserve to ourselves the right, should oppression or injustice be manifested in a warlike way by any of the European countries against them, and should they be unfortunate enough not to be able to give effective resistance, to determine whether it is not in our own interest to intervene and prevent an overturning of their government or an appropriation of their territory. But we recognize that this possibility is so remote that it practically removes them from the operation of the Monroe Doctrine. I am glad to see that Mr. Roosevelt, in his visit to those countries, has sought to impress them with the same view of the Monroe Doctrine that I have thus expressed. Indeed, he would have helped them, and us, too, far more if he had confined his teachings and lectures to explanations and limitations of the Monroe Doctrine and had not sought to destroy the independence of the judiciary and demoralize the administration of justice in two continents.

But it is said that we ought to invite in these so-called A B C powers of South America to assist us in upholding the Doctrine and also in doing what the Doctrine, as well as neighborhood interests, may lead us to do with near-by countries around the Gulf of Mexico and the Caribbean Sea.

It is suggested that we ought to establish some sort of relationship with these great powers as members of a kind of hegemony to decide upon Latin-American questions and participate in intervention to help along the smaller countries, and thus put such powers on an equality with us in our American policy and give assurance of our disinterestedness. If we could do this I would be glad to have it done, because it would relieve us of part of a burden and would give greater weight to the declaration of the policy. I would be glad to have an effort tactfully made to this end and I don't want to discourage it; but I fear we should find that these Powers would be loath to assume responsibility or burden in the matter of the welfare of a government like one of the Central American republics, or Haiti or Santo Domingo so remote from them and so near to us. We attempted, in case of disturbance in the Central American governments once or twice, to interest Mexico, when Mexico had a responsible government and was very near at hand, but President Diaz was loath to take any part with the United States in such an arrangement, and we found that whatever had to be done had to be done largely on the responsibility of the United States.

If action in respect of any republic of South America were necessary under the Monroe Doctrine, the joining of the A B C powers with the United States might involve suspicion and jealousy on the part of other South American republics not quite so prosperous or so stable as the A B C powers. Thus, instead of helping the situation, the participation of part of the South American governments might only complicate it. I know something about the character of those countries myself, not from personal observation but from a study of the character of Spanish-descended civilizations and societies, and I venture to say that, sensitive as they all may be in respect to suspected encroachments of the United States, they are even more sensitive as between themselves and their respective ambitions. During my administration Mr. Knox, the secretary of state, tendered the good offices of the United States as between South American governments who were bitter against each other over boundaries and other disputes, and successfully brought them to a peaceful solution; but in those controversies it was quite apparent that whatever might be the general feeling against the United States, their suspicions of each other, when their interests were at variance, were quite as intense. Indeed, it is not too much to say that the fear in the hearts of the less powerful peoples of South America of a South

American hegemony is more real than any genuine fear they may have of the actual suzerainty of our government. My belief, therefore, is that unless we could organize a union of all the countries of two continents, which would be so clumsy as to be entirely impracticable, the influence of the United States can probably be exerted in support of the Monroe Doctrine more effectively and much less invidiously alone than by an attempt to unite certain of the South American powers in an effort to preserve its successful maintenance. I hope my fear in this respect will prove to be unfounded and that the plan suggested may be successful.

I have read with a great deal of interest the account given by Professor Bingham of South American public opinion toward the United States in his most interesting book, which he calls "The Monroe Doctrine, an Obsolete Shibboleth." His views were based on an extended and very valuable opportunity for observation in nearly all the South American countries. He pictures with great force the feeling that is cultivated by the press of those countries against the United States, the deep suspicion that the people of South America have toward her professions of disinterestedness in South American and Central American politics, and their resentment at what they regard as an assumption of guardianship and of suzerainty over them, and a patronizing attitude which they believe to be involved in the maintenance of the Monroe Doctrine. He sets out the construction put by them on the various acts of the United States, and the mean and selfish and greedy motives they attribute to her, judging from speeches by their statesmen and politicians and from editorials of their newspapers. I know something of the opportunity the Spanish language affords to convey, with the most studied and graceful periods and with an assumption of courteous and impartial treatment, insinuations and suspicions of the sincerity of a person or a government against whom the writer desires to awaken the hostility of his readers. Professor Bingham, without discussing the merits of the acts of authorities of the United States, to which he invites attention, merely gives the view that the South American press of different countries took of those acts. No one can read the book and not see how unjust is much of the criticism of the United States. Nevertheless, I quite agree that it is the bounden duty of this government and her people to avoid as much as possible those acts which can give rise to a misconstruction of her motives, and to take a course which shall deprive them of any appearance of a desire to use her power in this hemisphere or to enforce and extend the Monroe Doctrine with a view to her selfish aggrandizement. I know the attractiveness of the Spanish-American; I know his high-born courtesy; I know his love of art, his poetic nature, his response to generous treatment; and I know how easily he misunderstands the thoughtless bluntness of an Anglo-Saxon diplomacy and the too frequent lack of regard for the feelings of others that we have inherited. I sympathize deeply with every effort to remove every obstacle to good feeling between us and a great and growing people, if only we are not called upon in doing so to give up something valuable to us and to the world.

The injustice of the attitude which Professor Bingham and others who take his views describe as that of the South American press may be seen by one or two references. Our Cuban war was begun with the most unselfish motives on our part and with a self-denying declaration; but it has been flaunted in South America as a war for aggrandizement and the exploitation of new territory, because the people of Puerto Rico desired to come under our government and we accepted them, and because we found the Philippines in such a condition of anarchy that we had to take them over. We have not exploited either Puerto Rico or the Philippines. We have only given them a better government and more prosperity and individual liberty than they ever had. We have promised the Filipinos that when their people acquire sufficient education and knowledge to make their government stable we will turn over the government to them. Twice Cuba has been under our control, and twice we have turned the island back to the people to whom we promised to do so when we entered upon the war. It has cost us hundreds of millions of money and many valuable lives to give her her independence. Nevertheless, our conduct, as unselfish and self-sacrificing as history shows, is treated among the South American people as an indication of our desire to enlarge our territorial control. Had we desired to extend our territory, how easily we could have done it? How many opportunities have been presented to us that we have rejected? Now, is it a reason for us to give up a doctrine that has for near a century helped along the cause of peace that our motives in maintaining it have been misconstrued by the peoples who have so much profited by our enforcing it? If we had entered upon the policy merely because those peoples asked us to assert it, and for no other reason, then their wish to end it might properly be given great weight, but the doctrine was originally declared to be one in our own interest and for our own safety. True, it has greatly strengthened our insistence upon the doctrine that it helped these peoples to maintain their governmental integrity and independence. Nevertheless, the question whether we shall continue it ought not to be controlled by their unjust feeling that our continued maintenance of the doctrine, with its proper limitations, in our own interest is in some way or other a reflection upon their national prestige and international standing. It has made for peace in ninety years. Why will it not make for peace the next one hundred years?

But it is said that the doctrine has been greatly extended and that it has led to intermeddling by our government in the politics of the smaller countries like Santo Domingo and the Central American republics, and that we are exercising a protectorate of a direct character over some of them. What we are doing with respect to them is in the interest of civilization, and we ought to do it to aid our neighboring governments whether the Monroe Doctrine prevails or not. My hope, as an earnest advocate of world peace, is that ultimately by international agreement we shall establish a court, like that of The Hague, into which any government aggrieved by any other government may bring the offending government before an impartial tribunal to answer for its fault and to abide the judgment of the court. Now, it is utterly impossible that the peace of the world may be brought about under such an arrangement as long as there are governments that cannot maintain peace within their own borders and whose instability is such that war is rather the normal than the exceptional status within their territory. One of the most crying needs in the cause of general peace is the promotion of stability in government in badly governed territory. This has been the case with Santo Domingo and Haiti. It has been true in a majority of the republics of Central America and until recently was true in the northern part of South America. Revolutions in those countries have been constant, peace has been the exception, and prosperity, health, happiness, law and order have all been impossible under such conditions and in such governments. The nearer they are to our borders the more of a nuisance they have become to us and the more injurious they are to our national interests. It was the neighborhood nuisance that led to the Cuban war and justified it. Now, when we properly may, with the consent of those in authority in such governments and without too much sacrifice on our part, aid those governments in bringing about stability and law and order, without involving ourselves in their civil wars, it is proper national policy for us to do so. It is not only proper national policy but it is international philanthropy. We owe it as much as the fortunate man owes aid to the unfortunate in the same neighborhood and in the same community. We are international trustees of the prosperity we have and the power we enjoy, and we are in duty bound to use them when it is both convenient and proper to help our neighbors. When this help prevents the happening of events that may prove to be an acute violation of the Monroe Doctrine by European governments, our duty in this regard is only increased and amplified. Therefore it was that Mr. Roosevelt mediated between Venezuela and the governments of England, Germany, and Italy, as I have already explained. So it was in the case of Santo Domingo, where a similar situation was foreshadowed, and in which, in order to relieve that situation, we assumed the burden of appointing tax-collectors and custom-house officials who were under our protection and who were saved from revolutionary attacks. We thus took away any motive for revolution, because it could not be successful without the funds which the seizure of custom-houses and the instrumentalities for the collection of taxes would furnish. This arrangement has been most profitable to the people of Santo Domingo and has relieved them from a succession of revolutions that had been their fate before it was adopted. The policy does not involve and ought not to involve a protectorate or any greater intervention in their internal affairs or a control of them than this power to protect custom-houses may involve. This is ample to secure pacification.

We cannot be too careful to avoid forcing our own ideas of government on peoples who, though favoring popular government, have such different ideas as to what constitutes it, and whose needs in respect to the forms of government that promote prosperity and happiness for them are widely variant from our own requirements.

Arrangements similar to that made with Santo Domingo were sought from the United States by the governments of Honduras and Nicaragua, and treaties were made, but they were defeated by the Senate of the United States without good ground, as it seems to me. I am glad to note that the present administration is looking with more favor upon treaties of this kind than its present supporters in the Senate were willing to give them when they were tendered to them for ratification by a Republican administration.

When we come to Mexico, where anarchy seems now to reign, the question is a most delicate one. Intervention by force means the expenditure of enormous treasure on our part, the loss of most valuable lives, and the dragging out of a tedious war against guerillas, in a trackless country, which will arouse no high patriotic spirit and which, after we have finished it and completed the work of tranquillity, will leave us still a problem full of difficulty and danger. All that those of us who are not in the government can do is to support the hands of the President and the secretary of state, and to present to the European powers and the world a solid front, with the prayer that the policy which is being pursued, whatever it may be, will be a successful one and relieve us from the awful burden of such a war as that I have described. In spite of the discouraging conditions in Mexico, however, the present situation illustrates the influence of the Monroe Doctrine on the attitude of the European powers, which, in spite of the injury to the property and persons of their nationals, look to the United States as the guide whom they are willing to follow in working out a solution. The condition of Mexico is bad enough, to be sure, but if it had involved us in European complications, such as would have been likely to arise had there been European intervention, its consequences might have been a great deal worse.

Exception is taken to the resolution which the Senate adopted in August, 1912, in which it was declared:

> That when any harbor or other place on the American continents is so situated that the occupation thereof for naval or military purposes might threaten the communications or the safety of the United States, the government of the United States could not see without grave concern the possession of such harbor or other place by any corporation or association which has such a relation to another government, not American, as to give that government practical power of control for national purposes.

It suffices to say that this is not an enlargement of the Monroe Doctrine. It only calls special attention to a way of indirection by which it can be violated. The policy of making this announcement at the time may perhaps be questioned, but that such an indirect method of securing a military outpost threatening to the safety of the United States would be injurious to her interests does not admit of doubt.

I do not intend here to go into the question of the merits of the controversy over the justice of our acquisition of the Canal Zone, enabling us to construct the Panama Canal. It would involve too long a discussion and is not relevant to the subject-matter of this chapter, because what was done in that case by our government was not any assertion of the Monroe Doctrine, was not justified on the ground of the Monroe Doctrine, and our right to do what we did was based on very different principles. Earnest and sincere efforts were made in my administration to satisfy the United States of Colombia. A treaty was made with her representative, in Mr. Roosevelt's administration, which seemed fair, but it was immediately rejected. All efforts to secure an adjustment of her grievances have failed, and recently negotiations were postponed by her, with the belief that the incoming administration, of different political complexion, would be more willing than mine to do what she regards as exact justice to her. We should, therefore, await with hope that the present administration may solve what for us was an insoluble difficulty.

Mr. Root, whose great constructive labors in the cause of world peace have just received most just recognition in the Nobel Prize, in his visit to South America attempted to convince the people of those republics that we wish no more territory and that we wish only the prosperity of all our neighbors. And Mr. Knox, in his visit to Venezuela and to all the republics of the West Indies and Central America, made the same effort. I hope that Mr. Roosevelt may carry the same message to South America. Doubtless, he is doing so.

After some years I hope that a consistent course on our part may effect an abatement of the present feeling described by Professor Bingham and others. But, however that may be, and whatever injustice the South American peoples may do us in suspecting us of selfish plans against them and their territory, we ought not to allow the present expressed hostility to the Monroe Doctrine, which really involves no assertion of suzerainty or sovereignty over them, to change our course. The doctrine is based on a wise policy in our own interest to exclude from this hemisphere the selfish political interference of European governments and their appropriation of territory, not for the purpose of increasing our power or territory, but for the purpose of promoting the prosperity, independence, and happiness of the peoples of these two continents and so of insuring our own peace and safety.

2

Shall the Federal Government Protect Aliens in
Their Treaty Rights?

The spread of democracy throughout the world and the influence that each
people has in determining the foreign policy of its government have necessarily affected the discussion of useful agencies for the avoidance of war.
Before the nineteenth century, wars largely turned upon the interests of
dynasties and the ambitions and hatreds of kings, but now wars between
countries having stable governments are rarely begun without the wish of
the majority of their respective peoples. Even a country like Russia, in the
government of which the people are not supposed to have a great voice,
was obliged to make peace in the Japanese war largely because her people
opposed its continuance. Therefore, it becomes important, in the maintenance of peace, that each stable government representing its people in its
foreign relations, and being answerable for them to another people, should
be able to perform its promises promptly, and should certainly not keep
them only to the ear and break them to the hope. Nice distinctions based
on precedents in international law have more weight with learned statesmen representing a dynasty than with an angered people. When they suffer
injustice they look to the substance of the international contract for their

protection, and if that is not performed, and the breach is an outrage upon their own race and their own kith and kin, their indignant feeling is dangerous to the peace between the two nations.

In one of my visits to Japan, as secretary of war, I had the pleasure of meeting and talking with Count Hayashi, one of the great statesmen and diplomats of that wonderful empire, and recently deceased. We were discussing very freely the relations between Japan and the United States, and he said that he felt confident that I was right in saying that the United States had no desire for a war with Japan, but, on the contrary, wished to avoid it by every honorable means. He expressed the hope that I credited his statement that the empire of Japan and those responsible for its government were equally anxious to make the peace between the two countries permanent and abiding. "But," said he, "my people have grown much in national stature. They have won successes, civil and military. They have a deep love of their country and of their fellow countrymen, and perhaps they have what you will call 'patriotic self-conceit.' However this may be, their sensitiveness as a nation has increased, and it makes them deeply resent an injustice or an invidious discrimination against them in a foreign country or by a foreign people. The only possible danger of a breach between our two nations that I can imagine would be one growing out of the mistreatment of our people, living under the promised protection of the United States, through the lawless violence of a mob directed against them as Japanese."

Now, what is true of the relation of these two countries is likely to be true of the relation between the United States and peoples of other countries. With almost every nation we have a treaty in which each contracting party agrees that the nationals of the other party may reside within its jurisdiction and, complying with the laws, may legally pursue their vocations or business and enjoy the same protection to life, liberty, and property that the citizens of the contracting country enjoy. This is, perhaps, the most common clause in the many treaties of amity and commerce that now control the relations between the nations of the world.

Since 1811 there have been many cases of mob violence against aliens, in which they have been killed or grievously injured. And while in all these cases we denied any liability, Congress has generally made payments to those who were injured and to the families of those who were killed. In some cases the amount paid was recited in the act of appropriation to be a gratuity without admission of liability. In other cases the amount was paid without such reservation. In no case that I have been able to discover have the perpetrators of these outrages been punished. In all the cases the local authorities have evidently sympathized with the mob spirit and purpose or have been so terrorized by it as to avoid making a judicial investigation of real thoroughness. The results have thus been: first, the mob; second, the felonious assault, or murder, and destruction of property; third, the farce of a State investigation; fourth, the indemnity to the injured and the family of the dead; and, fifth, the complete immunity of the guilty. Such a list of outrages, reaching clear from 1811 down to 1910, without punishment, is not a record in which we can take pride.

I propose to consider here whether anything can be done to change this state of affairs so long continued that recurring incidents of the same kind constitute it a custom. I feel confident that something effective can be done to this end through valid federal legislation conferring on the federal government and courts executive and judicial jurisdiction to prevent and punish these crimes against aliens in violation of their treaty rights.

In some of such cases the feeling between the countries involved has run high, and with the increased popular control of foreign policies we may expect these incidents to become more dangerous to our peace. In letters of our secretaries of state, in answer to complaints of foreign governments in such cases, attention is called to the fact that our general government has no jurisdiction to direct the prosecution under federal law of the perpetrators of these outrages, and the secretaries have been content with the statement that the persons killed or injured have had the same protection that citizens of this country have had, which, I may add, in all the instances under examination, was no protection at all. The secretaries have pointed out that if protection was needed or punishment was to be inflicted, it was the duty of the State authorities to give it, as would have been the case had the persons killed or feloniously assaulted been American citizens. We make a promise and then we let somebody else attempt to perform it, and when it is not performed and it never is, we say: "We are not responsible for this. It is somebody else's failure, and, besides, you are not suffering any worse than our own citizens in this matter, because they enjoy the same absence of protection extended to your people. However, say no more about it. We'll salve your feelings by a little money, the amount of which we'll fix." Now, we know the fact to be from this history that in such cases generally there is not the slightest hope through the State courts of having proper punishment inflicted, or even attempted. In such cases the juries are generally drawn from the immediate neighborhood of the county and town in which the outrage is committed, and the case ultimately reduces itself to the result that the grand jury, or, if an indictment is found, which is almost as rare as a conviction, the petit jury, will be composed of either the criminals themselves or of their relatives and neighbors and sympathizers, and the prosecution is a farce.

It does not soothe one's pride of country to note the number of lynchings of our own citizens that go unwhipped of justice and that are properly held up to us with scorn whenever we assume, as we too frequently do, a morality higher than, and a government better than, that of other peoples. Nor is our feeling in this regard rendered less acute by hearing from the governors of some of our States expressions brazenly defending and approving such lynchings. Still more embarrassing is our situation, when we are called upon to explain to a government with which we have made a solemn covenant to protect its citizens or subjects in their right of peaceable residence here and in the enjoyment of business and happiness under the ægis of the United States, that, while we did make a covenant, it ought to have known that under our system we as a government had no means of performing that covenant or of punishing those who, as our citizens, had grossly violated it. For lynchings of our own citizens within the jurisdiction of the State we can say to ourselves, for we have no other plea, that under the form of our government such crimes are a State matter, and if the people of a State will not provide, for their own protection, a machinery in the administration of justice that will prevent such lawless violence, and a public opinion to make it effective, then it is for them to bear the ignominy of such a condition. But when, in the case of the lynchings of aliens, whom we have plighted our national faith to protect, the fact is that the Federal Government has the power to enact legislation to set its own administration of justice going by its own prosecuting officers and through its own courts, and has not done so, we may well hang our heads in the face of adverse criticism.

Such legislation need not find its only reason in our pride of country and our commendable desire to be considered in the first rank of civilized nations, observant of treaty obligations and earnest in the protection of the rights both of our own citizens and our foreign guests. A much stronger reason for such legislation is in the Federal Government's taking over the right to protect itself and all the people against the danger of war that may be thrust on us by the lawless, cruel, prejudiced action of the people of a town, a city, or a county in dealing with subjects or citizens of other countries. It might well be that the race prejudice of such a community would carry us into war, and thus sacrifice thousands of valuable citizens drawn from the whole country, and consume hundreds of millions of treasure, to be met by taxation upon all the people of the United States. Ought not the government, therefore, to insist, should not all the people of the United States require, that their executive at Washington, with a full knowledge of our delicate relations to the foreign sovereign whose subjects have been murdered, should have power enough to set the whole prosecuting and detective machinery of the government at work to bring the ringleaders of such mobs to trial before juries summoned from a wider vicinage than that of the local community in which the outrage was committed, and free from the sympathy and terrorism there likely to exist?

But it is said that the dead are not protected or restored to life by punishment of the malefactors, that those who are injured have no right to criminal prosecutions, which are matters of State concern only, and that, as the injury has been done, if pecuniary indemnity is granted by the general government, all that the victims can properly demand is given them. I am not discussing this from the standpoint of the victims at all. I am discussing it from the standpoint of our own governmental self-respect, safety, and freedom from international offence. It is true that the only punishment of perpetrators to such an outrage must come after the outrage; but if the ringleaders of one mob in a United States court were hanged for murder, the number of future lynchings of foreigners would be reduced in direct ratio to the certainty of a repetition of that kind of justice. I have had occasion to say before, and I say again, that the manner of trial in the Federal courts, in which the judge has the same control of the trial that he has at common law, can assist the jury in its investigation of facts, and can take charge of the trial out of the hands of the counsel for the defence, is a terror to evil-doers. While in the Eastern State courts, justice in crimes of

violence is generally meted out with even hand, in the Western and South-
ern State courts this is not true, and the difference between the administration in the Federal courts and in the State courts in such States is well
known to those who are likely to become criminals. The certainty with
which mail robbers have been brought to justice makes every man who
thinks of robbing the mail consider the chances of escape from Uncle Sam.
Indeed, cases have occurred in which train robbers have religiously re-
frained from sacking the mail-car in order to avoid the federal jurisdiction.
Moreover, in cases of mob violence against aliens, the direct energetic action of the National Government under the eye of the complaining foreign
ambassador at Washington would itself take the sting out of the incident,
and minimize its danger as a cause for bad feeling between the two countries.

Of course, every one recognizes that the government of the United
States cannot guarantee the detection and arrest of the criminals in such
cases, or contract that when they are caught and tried, conviction will necessarily follow. In no civilized country can this be assured, and this circum-
stance is an implied term of every treaty promise of this sort. But that
uncertainty does not prevent courage, promptness, and energy on the part
of the marshals and detective agents of the government in efforts to identify
and arrest the offenders and to find the evidence against them, or efficiency
on the part of the prosecuting officers in properly preparing the case for
the grand and petit juries. It is the utter absence of any sincere effort of the
local authorities in such cases to bring the criminals to justice that naturally
angers foreign peoples when they are asking reparation for the awful results
of mob violence. It is our actual helplessness, and our hopelessness of any
remedial measures to prevent a recurrence of such outrages, that give the
futile negotiation such a deplorable color in the eyes of the injured nation.

We can all remember the deep feeling aroused in our whole people
over the massacre of the Jews in parts of Russia and the intense indignation
that manifested itself among their coreligionists in this country, and how
sceptical all our people were concerning official denials of governmental
responsibility for such outrages. Let us try to look at lynchings of aliens in
this country from the standpoint of their fellow countrymen at home. In
the utter absence of protection or attempted punishment of the murderers,
can we wonder that there should be a deep-seated suspicion on their part

that the bloody riots have been with either the connivance or acquiescence of our authorities?

Federal legislation which would remedy the present great defect in the powers of the National Government to protect aliens in their treaty rights has been proposed to Congress a number of times and has encountered serious opposition. The question was submitted to a committee of the American Bar Association that made a report in 1892, in which the constitutionality of such legislation was doubted and its wisdom was vigorously denied. We must assume that the reasons stated by the committee in that report are those which have moved Congress to withhold the action for which, in my judgment, there is a crying need. It is greater now than ever it was. It cannot be said that respect for the law or constituted authority has increased in this country. Especially has it been weakened in those communities where class or race feeling seeks expression. Nor is the administration of criminal justice in the States in such cases likely to be more prompt or certain in the future than in the past. It is in such jurisdictions that the innovation of recall of executive officers is in vogue—a device which is not calculated to make governors or sheriffs or prosecuting attorneys more active in their arrest and prosecution of mob leaders, who are too often only exponents of local feeling and have the sympathy of the vicinage. When we add, as we may, that in many such States the recall of judges also has just come into use, we can understand how utterly futile it is to expect that there will be any improvement in making good the government's promise to aliens through such official agencies.

In order to meet the arguments of those who oppose this legislation, I shall run over the objections that were presented by the committee of the American Bar Association to whose report I have referred. I ought to say in advance, with respect to the committee, that it was evidently composed of strict constructionists of the Constitution, that their report was not adopted by the American Bar Association, but that instead they were discharged from the consideration of the subject, and, because of divided views in the association, a resolution was adopted declaring it inexpedient for the association to make any recommendation to Congress on the subject. The reference of the subject to the committee was prompted by the then recent lynching of nine Italians confined in a New Orleans jail. A bill had been introduced into Congress to confer on Federal courts jurisdiction to try and punish perpetrators of such outrages.

The first reason given as against such legislation was that outrages equally shocking as that at New Orleans had occurred in the past without suggesting any necessity for interfering with the powers of the States to punish crime. It might have been added that no one had ever been brought to justice for the commission of any of the outrages of a similar character that had been committed since 1811. Just because a glaring defect has been allowed to exist for a century, is that any reason why we should not now take steps to remedy it?

The second objection was that in more than a century only seven cases have occurred to which by any possibility this legislation could apply.

In answer to this, I can only set out an official list of the outrages committed in recent years.

At Rock Springs, Wyoming, on November 30, 1885, there was an armed attack by one hundred men on a Chinese settlement in a mining town, in which all the houses were burnt, and in which twenty-eight Chinamen lost their lives, sixteen were wounded, and all their property was destroyed.

In a similar attack in Squak Valley, Washington, three Chinamen were killed and four wounded.

At Orofino, in Idaho, five Chinese were killed.

At Anaconda, in Montana, four Chinamen were killed.

At Snake River, Oregon, ten Chinamen were killed.

In Juneau, Alaska, one hundred Chinese were expelled by lawless violence from their homes and the territory.

In an official note of February 15, 1886, riots were reported at Bloomfield, Redding, Boulder Creek, Eureka, and other towns in California, involving murder, arson, and robbery, and it was added that thousands of Chinese had been driven from their homes.

Nine Italians were lynched in New Orleans in 1891.

In August, 1895, one Mexican was lynched in California.

In October, 1895, one Mexican was lynched in Texas.

In 1895 three Italians were lynched at Walsenberg, Colorado.

In 1896 three Italians were lynched at Hahnville, Louisiana.

In 1899 three Italians were lynched at Tallulah, Louisiana.

In 1901 three Italians were lynched at Erin, Mississippi.

In 1910 one Italian was lynched in Florida.

This list, it seems to me, is a sufficient answer to the suggestion made by the committee that such events do not occur with sufficient frequency to require reform, especially when we consider in connection with these cases the recent very acute feeling over the treatment of Japanese subjects in California.

The third objection by the committee to Federal control of such prosecutions was that two of the outrages against aliens were in territories in control of the Federal Government, and no better enforcement of the law was shown there than in State jurisdiction. They were in territories under the control of territorial governments, with the same weaknesses that a State government has, with prosecutions in a county, with the jury drawn from the immediate vicinage and under the terrorism of a small locality, which is a very different thing from prosecutions in the regular Federal courts.

The committee's fourth objection was that the suggestion of this legislation has not come in any case from a foreign power with whom we are in treaty relations, and that the demands pressed upon the United States Government have been almost uniformly not so much for punishment of the assailants as for pecuniary indemnity, which the injured parties had already the right to seek in the United States courts.

This statement is inaccurate. In many of the instances in which extended correspondence was had with our State department by the diplomatic representative of the foreign governments whose subjects had been killed or injured there were demands for punishment, and there were suggestions that the promise of protection was made by the United States in the treaty and that the foreign countries looked to the United States and not to the subordinate States for compliance with treaty obligations.

The fifth objection was that our secretaries of state, in their correspondence with complaining foreign representatives, have uniformly insisted upon the common-law principle that the punishment of crime must be left to the ordinary and orderly administration of justice by the State courts in like manner as in similar cases affecting our own citizens.

Of course our government has taken that position. The secretaries of state found themselves in such a position that they had to. It is not to be expected that they would have made prominent our failure to legislate when we might have legislated to give us the proper means of discharging our obligations.

In his annual message of December 5, 1899, President McKinley used these words:

> For the fourth time in the present decade question has arisen with the Government of Italy in regard to the lynching of Italian subjects. The latest of these deplorable events occurred at Tallulah, Louisiana, whereby five unfortunates of Italian origin were taken from jail and hanged. . . . The recurrence of these distressing manifestations of blind mob fury directed at dependents or natives of a foreign country suggests that the contingency has arisen for action by Congress in the direction of conferring upon the federal courts jurisdiction in this class of international cases where the ultimate responsibility of the Federal Government may be involved.

And he refers to a recommendation of President Harrison made in this matter in 1891, just after the Mafia case, in which President Harrison said: "It would, I believe, be entirely competent for Congress to make offenses against the treaty rights of foreigners domiciled in the United States cognizable in the federal courts. This has not, however, been done, and the federal officers and courts have no power in such cases to intervene either for the protection of a foreign citizen or for the punishment of his slayers."

President McKinley then said: "I earnestly recommend that the subject be taken up anew and acted upon during the present session. The necessity for some such provision abundantly appears."

In his message of 1900 the same President made another urgent recommendation of the same kind.

President Roosevelt, in his annual message of December, 1906, in dealing with our relations with Japan, which were then of much public concern, said:

> One of the great embarrassments attending the performance of our international obligations is the fact that the statutes of the United States are entirely inadequate. They fail to give to the national government sufficiently ample power, through United States courts and by the use of the army and navy, to protect aliens in the rights secured to them

under solemn treaties which are the law of the land. I, therefore, earnestly recommend that the criminal and civil statutes of the United States be so amended and added to as to enable the President, acting for the United States Government, which is responsible in our international relations, to enforce the rights of aliens under treaties. There should be no particle of doubt as to the power of the national government completely to perform and enforce its own obligations to other nations. The mob of a single city may at any time perform acts of lawless violence against some class of foreigners which would plunge us into war. That city by itself would be powerless to make defense against the foreign power thus assaulted, and if independent of this government it would never venture to perform or permit the performance of the acts complained of. The entire power and the whole duty to protect the offending city or the offending community lies in the hands of the United States Government. It is unthinkable that we should continue a policy under which a given locality may be allowed to commit a crime against a friendly nation, and the United States Government limited, not to preventing the commission of the crime, but, in the last resort, to defending the people who have committed it against the consequences of their own wrong-doing.

And in my Inaugural address, March 4, 1909, I brought the subject to the attention of Congress as strongly as I could, as follows:

> By proper legislation we may, and ought to, place in the hands of the federal executive the means of enforcing the treaty rights of such aliens in the courts of the Federal Government. It puts our government in a pusillanimous position to make definite engagements to protect aliens and then to excuse the failure to perform those engagements by an explanation that the duty to keep them is in States or cities, not within our control. If we would promise we must put ourselves in a position to perform our promise. We cannot permit the possible failure of justice, due to local prejudice in any State or municipal government, to expose us to the risk of a war which might be avoided if Federal jurisdiction was asserted by suitable legislation by Congress and carried out by proper proceedings instituted by the executive in the courts of the national government.

These citations would seem to refute any suggestion that those having official responsibility for our foreign relations have not realized the crying need for such legislation.

The committee's sixth objection was that upon this basis all complaints arising out of such cases have been settled through the ordinary diplomatic channels and without any loss of self-respect to our government

That is a matter of opinion. If one can judge from the communications from some of the secretaries of state to Congress and the messages of the Presidents just quoted, they feel very deeply the loss of self-respect that their enforced attitude and their inability to take action involves. Indeed, it is impossible to explain the payment by the Congress of the United States, on the recommendation by the executive, of an indemnity in every case of these international outrages, unless there has been a real feeling on the part of the authorities of this government that we are at fault and that we intend to do something to save, as much as possible, the blame that is properly chargeable to us and our government. The position of the government usually is that we do not owe anything as a matter of right. If so, and if it is sound doctrine that we must treat equally the citizens of our own country and citizens of a foreign country, why should we discriminate and pay an indemnity to the foreign citizens or subjects who were injured or killed and not pay a similar indemnity in cases of lynchings of our own citizens? Our position and our action are not consistent and the reason why they are not consistent is because we have made the promise and are not in a position to perform it, and therefore we do the next best thing and try to salve the wounds of our sister nations by money payments.

The committee's seventh objection was that the method of dealing with such cases in England, the other great common-law country, is precisely analogous to our own.

This is inaccurate because in England the initiation of the administration of justice, the detection of criminals, and the control of their prosecution is with the law officers of the crown.

Then the learned committeemen went into a consideration of the possible anomalies that would arise were felonious assaults upon foreign subjects or citizens made a federal offence. It was said that it might involve double jeopardy. Well, there are a great many instances in which just such double jeopardy, if it can be called such, occurs in respect of acts that constitute an offence against both State and Federal sovereignties. In view of the fact that such offences are never brought to trial in a State, much less to conviction, the practical danger of double jeopardy, if it be such, is most remote.

Then it is said that it will produce great confusion because there are so many aliens in this country that the assaults upon whom would crowd the Federal courts and introduce a deplorable delay.

Even if there were some delay in finally disposing of such cases, their energetic initiation is much to be preferred to that kind of despatch of the business in State courts which results in a report of the coroner and grand jury that the perpetrators are unknown. Nor is it true that such cases would clog the Federal courts. Those courts can take care of many more criminal cases today than in 1891, and the discretion of the attorney-general or the prosecuting officer of the Federal Government can well be trusted to leave to the jurisdiction of the State courts those crimes of violence against aliens that are in ordinary course and do not really involve race or national feeling or international complications. There are many classes of offences cognizable in both Federal and State jurisdictions in which such comity of arrangement exists and is satisfactory in its operation.

But it is suggested that in some way or other we are putting the foreigners into a privileged class by providing for their protection by the United States courts and United States officers. Don't we do so by paying indemnities? But, more than this, the suggestion is beside the mark. Criminals have no vested rights to trial in a jurisdiction where conviction is impossible, or to object to a jurisdiction which is likely to convict them when they assault those whom the plighted hospitality of the nation ought to protect. We are not putting the victims in a privileged class solely or chiefly for the purpose of giving them any benefit, but rather for the purpose of protecting the Federal Government from just complaint by a sister nation and from being possibly involved in war by the lawlessness and selfishness of local communities.

The reasons of legislative policy advanced by the committee against the bill were thus, in the highest degree, technical and entirely without weight, and the lamentable occurrences since their report emphasize their error.

Finally, the committee intimated that such legislation as proposed would be in violation of the Constitution. They do not argue this out. They only suggest that it would be an invasion of the police power of the

States, and they assume a construction of the Constitution that would have done in the days of Chief Justice Taney and the strict construction period of the Supreme Court before the war. They ignore a specific declaration by the Supreme Court that such legislation would be valid and a long series of cases by that tribunal which by analogy leave not the slightest doubt of the power of the government not only to assume such judicial jurisdiction after the offence, but also to take preventive executive measures before the offence to stop such outrages.

The bill proposed to give jurisdiction of such cases to the federal courts is as follows:

> Be it enacted by the Senate and House of Representatives of the United States of America, in Congress assembled, that any act committed in any state or territory of the United States in violation of the rights of a citizen or subject of a foreign country secured to such citizen or subject by treaty between the United States and such foreign country, which act constitutes a crime under the laws of such state or territory, shall constitute a like crime against the peace and dignity of the United States, punishable in like manner as in the courts of said state or territory, and within the period limited by the laws of such state or territory, and may be prosecuted in the courts of the United States, and, upon conviction, the sentence executed in like manner as sentences upon convictions for crimes under the laws of the United States.

The question of the validity of this proposed legislation under the Constitution involves a consideration of the treaty-making power of the Federal Government and the powers necessarily resultant from that and incident to it.

The treaty-making power of the United States is the widest power that it has. The executive power in our domestic field of government is divided between the general government and the State governments, between the President and other executive officers of the United States, on the one hand, and State governors and other executive officers of the States on the other. The legislative power is divided between Congress and the legislatures of the States. The judicial power is divided between the Federal courts that exercise the jurisdiction extended to them by the Federal Constitution and laws and the courts of the States. But all governmental power exercised by the country in dealing with foreign governments is exercised by the Federal Government alone, and the only limitation upon that power is that in treaty making the President and the Senate shall not violate any prohibition of the Constitution and shall exercise that power within the limits which international practice normally imposes as to the subjects to be included in a treaty. This wide and exclusive power of the central government in treaty making is easily to be inferred from the fact that by the Constitution the States are expressly forbidden to enter into any treaty, alliance, or confederation, to grant letters of marque and reprisal, unless Congress consents, to lay any duty of tonnage, to keep troops or ships of war, in time of peace, to enter into any agreement or compact with another State or with a foreign power, or to engage in war unless invaded; while the general government is expressly empowered to make treaties, to regulate commerce with foreign nations, to establish a uniform rule of naturalization, to define and punish piracies and felonies committed on the high seas, and offences against the law of nations, to declare war, grant letters of marque and reprisal, and make rules concerning captures on land or water, to raise and support armies, to provide and maintain a navy, to make rules for the government and regulation of the land and naval forces, to provide for the calling forth the militia to repel invasions, to appoint ambassadors and other public ministers and consuls, and to adjudicate causes arising under treaties and all cases affecting ambassadors, other public ministers, and consuls, causes of admiralty and maritime jurisdiction, and cases between a State or the citizens thereof, and foreign states, citizens, and subjects. And, further than this, the treaties made by the authority of the United States are expressly declared to be the supreme law of the land and the judges in every State are to be bound thereby, anything in the Constitution or the laws of any State to the contrary notwithstanding.

It would be difficult to make clearer the intention of the framers of the Constitution and the people who ratified it to give over to the general government the executive power to control foreign affairs and to give to the treaty-making power as wide a scope as treaties between independent governments are wont to have. As already said, one of the most common provisions in treaties between civilized countries is that which reciprocally binds each of the parties to give an opportunity for peaceful residence and pursuit of business in its territory to the citizens or subjects of the other.

Unlike treaties in most countries, a treaty made by the United States has a double aspect. It is not only a contract between the two countries, as it is in England and in other jurisdictions. It is that and more, because in so far as its provisions in their nature can have operation in the United States as municipal law, they are statutes. They are equivalent to a law passed by Congress, and as such they repeal a previous inconsistent law of Congress, on the one hand, and can be repealed by a subsequent inconsistent law of Congress on the other. It follows, therefore, that aliens living in this country, whose sovereign has made a treaty with the United States in which the United States guarantees protection to life and property to such aliens during their residence within the jurisdiction of the United States, have a right under the federal Constitution and law to be secure against any invasion of their peaceable residence and the holding of property. Under the eighteenth clause of Section VIII of Article I of the Constitution, Congress has power to make all laws which shall be necessary and proper for carrying into execution all powers vested by this Constitution in the government of the United States. It needs no straining of logic, but only the use of the reasoning pursued by the Supreme Court in hundreds of similar cases, to deduce the power of Congress under that clause to enact legislation to carry out and execute such an agreement by the United States to protect aliens from lawless violence. Therefore, it would be entirely competent for Congress to pass the bill I have quoted above.

Now, if the committee of the Bar Association, to which I have referred, had not expressed some doubts as to the power of Congress to pass such a law, I would not have thought it necessary to argue it. The power has been expressly affirmed by the Supreme Court. The case of *Baldwin vs. Franks,* 120 U.S. 678, involved the punishment of a man for using lawless violence against Chinese aliens resident in California, driving them from their residence and depriving them of their legitimate business, contrary to a treaty made between the United States and China in 1881.

The Supreme Court said: "That the treaty-making power has been surrendered by the States and given to the United States is unquestionable. It is true, also, that the treaties made by the United States and in force are part of the supreme law of the land, and that they are as binding within the territorial limits of the States as they are elsewhere throughout the dominion of the United States."

The court then recites the clause of the treaty and continues:

> That the United States have power under the Constitution to provide
> for the punishment of those who are guilty of depriving Chinese subjects
> of any of the rights, privileges, immunities, or exemptions guaranteed
> to them by this treaty, we do not doubt. What we have to decide, under
> the questions certified here from the court below, is whether this has
> been done by the sections of the revised statutes specially referred to.

But they found no law on the statute book with language which em-
braced such offences.

This decision was rendered in 1887 and the report of the Bar Association committee was in 1891, and the report, so far as I can find, does not
mention the decision of the court in *Baldwin vs. Franks.* As the committee
of the Bar Association had no jurisdiction to reverse the views of the Supreme Court, I assume that we can treat the constitutional construction
declared by the Supreme Court as still in force.

But such punishment of crime in the federal courts and by the authority of the United States against those who violate the treaty rights of aliens
is not the only thing that can be done. One of the ideas that it took a long
time to get into the heads of strict constructionists of the Constitution was
that there is not only the peace of a State, but there is also, on the same
soil, the peace of the United States; that while the breach of State law by
violence is a breach of the peace of the State, breadth of Federal law by
violence is a breach of the peace of the United States.

In the case of *Ex Parte Siebold,* 100 U.S. 371–394, the court was considering an objection, very similar to the one made here, against a law providing for the protection of a citizen of a State in his rights under the Federal
Constitution against assault. They said:

> It is argued that the preservation of peace and good order in society is
> not within the powers confided to the government of the United States,
> but belongs exclusively to the States. Here again we are met with the
> theory that the government of the United States does not rest upon the
> soil and territory of the country. We think that this theory is founded
> on an entire misconception of the nature and powers of that govern-
> ment. We hold it to be an incontrovertible principle that the govern-
> ment of the United States may, by means of physical force, exercised

through its official agents, execute on every foot of American soil the powers and functions that belong to it. This necessarily involves the power to command obedience to its law, and hence the power to keep the peace to that extent.

In the Debs case, reported in 158 U.S. 564, Mr. Justice Brewer said: "The entire strength of the nation may be used to enforce in any part of the land the full and free exercise of all national powers and the security of all rights entrusted by the Constitution to its care. . . . If the emergency arises, the army of the nation, and all its militia, are at the service of the nation to compel obedience to its laws."

This language has exact application to the protection of the treaty rights of aliens. Therefore, not only ought the bill to be passed which I have read above, providing for a punishment of lawless violence directed against the rights and welfare of aliens guaranteed in a treaty of the United States, but express statutory provision ought also to be made enabling the President, in his discretion, to act directly, and without reference to State action, in protection of such aliens when their safety and peaceable residence are threatened. Such executive power would doubtless be implied if Federal court jurisdiction were given, but it would be greatly better to make it express. Then the President could move at once to the protection of aliens living in settlements where mobs threaten attack, and practical results might be expected, making the protection of the United States a real thing. Then the secretary of state could look in the face the ambassador of the country whose subjects or citizens are threatened with a gross violation of their treaty rights, and point to the effective measures of protection taken to vindicate the honor and the plighted faith of the United States.

Now, if such legislation is so plainly needed, why has it not been enacted? This is a hard question for me to answer except by suggesting that aliens are not voters and their rights are not a political issue. Both parties are at fault in this matter. When I was President, as quoted above, I urged the adoption of such legislation, and then took such steps as I could in other ways to secure its enactment. At my suggestion, Mr. Swagar Sherley, a leading Democratic member of the House, from Louisville, Kentucky, attempted to introduce such legislation into the revision of the judicial code, but objection was made on the ground that it would introduce new legislation into a code that should be only a revision of existing legislation. The separate bill for the purpose which was introduced, I could not, in the pressure of other legislation, induce either House to take up. There seemed to be the strong opposition not only of Democrats from the South but of Republicans from the far West, and this prevented its consideration.

May we, therefore, not ask from this administration, in the course of which there has been exhibited, under the admirable leadership of the President, such wonderful party discipline in the passage of legislation, that action be taken on this important matter? The negotiations with Japan would, I am sure, be greatly assisted by giving such an earnest of the sincerity of our government in protecting her people in the rights we assure them. If it be said that the party in power is traditionally opposed to giving the Federal Government more functions and to concentration of power in Washington, we may well urge that when the party in power has swallowed camels in the passage of a law giving the largest government control of banking and currency known in our history, and in projecting a law vesting the widest Federal power in respect to corporations doing interstate business, and another looking to Federal regulation of presidential primaries, the party leaders should not strain at the gnat of Federal performance of Federal promises, even if it may involve the transfer to the jurisdiction of Federal courts of a comparatively few cases which are now in theory triable in State courts but in fact are never tried there.

3

Arbitration Treaties that Mean Something

The war between Italy and Tripoli, the war in China, the war between the Balkan States and Turkey and then the subsequent war between the Balkan States themselves, the war in Haiti, and finally the war in Mexico, all are contemporary and convincing evidence that the dawn of universal peace is not immediately at hand. It is true that these are nearly all of them civil wars or revolutions, and that the restoration of peace in most of them requires only the establishment of stable governments. It is very certain that in such cases, treaties of arbitration, whatever their terms and however solemnly entered into, are not a practical means of settlement. Many countries in the last century suffered from the disease of revolution. Looking back over half a century, we can properly say that in the countries subject to such outbreaks there has been great improvement; and, while Mexico shows retrogression in this regard, most of the South American countries have grown stronger in the maintenance of law and order and the preservation of constituted authority.

I think it is our duty, as a great, strong, powerful nation, when we can easily do so without involving ourselves in costly or dangerous war, to promote the cause of peace and order in any of our less stable neighbors through treaty arrangements with them, and this wholly without regard to the Monroe Doctrine. We have had such an opportunity with Nicaragua, with Honduras, with Santo Domingo, and we may possibly have the same kind of an opportunity with other states similarly conditioned. They all owe what to them is a large amount of money to European creditors. Their creditors are willing to scale down the debts, which in justice ought to be substantially scaled, if they can be given greater security. The governments of these countries, confident that we are disinterested in the matter, have manifested a desire to have American bankers finance the readjustment of their obligations if our government will only consent to a treaty in which there is reserved to us the right to nominate collectors of their customs revenues and to protect such collectors against lawless violence.

The amount of force necessary to extend this protection is almost negligible. Indeed, it is not more than the show of force that we usually make to protect American interests in the breaking out of a revolution in these countries. I never have been able to understand the argument against such treaties. They do not involve the Monroe Doctrine at all. They merely involve the obligation of a strong and powerful neighbor to help a weak one. They are in the interest of peace and good order and make for the just settlement of debts. In some way or other, such treaties are supposed to be a recognition of the right of European governments to collect the debts of their nationals by force; but I am unable to see why. They constitute merely a friendly act, and furnish a means to these governments of settling their past obligations and obtaining a much-needed sum of money to be expended in helping their people in education and in the development of their rich natural resources.

In Central America the difficulty has been that a dictator in one republic has intrigued against his neighbors. He became a disturbing factor for all the rest. The treaties with Honduras and Nicaragua would give the United States an opportunity to exert a direct influence to prevent the consummation of such intrigues and to maintain a peace in that region of North America essential to the happiness of its people. Their trade is naturally of great value to us, and would be of much greater value if the arts of peace were pursued.

But the subject of this chapter is not that of specific treaties. It is the question of the relation of the Senate to general arbitration treaties. I understand a general arbitration treaty to mean a treaty by which the nations who are parties to it agree that they will in the future submit to arbitration all future differences which come within a class of issues defined in the treaty. What I propose to discuss here is whether the President and the Senate have the power to make such treaties in a form that will really bind them and the government to anything substantial.

In Mr. Roosevelt's term there were a number of arbitration treaties negotiated and signed by Mr. Hay and submitted to the Senate, in which it was agreed between the United States and the other treaty-making party that all questions of a legal nature, not including those of national honor or vital interest, would be submitted to The Hague tribunal, and that when any difference arose a specific agreement of submission of the issue would be entered into. The Senate insisted that for the words "specific agreement," "treaty" should be substituted, in order that no specific agreement could be submitted under the treaty except with the advice and consent of the Senate. Mr. Roosevelt declined to ratify treaties with this limitation, on the ground that the treaty thus limited did not bring the country any nearer to arbitration than if no treaty was made. On the other hand, the Senate insisted that it had no power to ratify such a treaty because it would be an unlawful delegation to the President alone of the treaty-making power.

The treaties thus drawn either attempted to describe a class of questions which the government bound itself to arbitrate or they did not. If not, then they were not treaties at all, and there was no occasion to discuss what the Constitution required with reference to treaties. In that view they were a mere general declaratory expression of a hope that the parties might make a treaty in the future. If, however, the treaties did define a class of issues which the United States agreed to arbitrate, then whether an issue thereafter arising came within the class or not was a matter of construction of the treaty. The agreement would then be nothing more than the framing of the specific issue which came within the general class as defined. It is a well-understood incident of the treaty-making power that in a treaty there may be reserved, without an unlawful delegation of power, to the President, or to some other agent, the power to execute its provisions: As the

Supreme Court said in *Tong Yue Ting vs. the United States,* 149 U.S. 698 and 714:

> It is no new thing for the law-making power, acting either through treaties made by the President and the Senate, or by the more common methods of the acts of Congress, to submit the decision of questions not necessarily of judicial cognizance either to the final determination of executive officers, or to the decisions of such officers in the first instance, with such opportunity for judicial review of their action as Congress may see fit to authorize and permit.

It was, therefore, entirely within the authority of the treaty-making power, after having laid down a general rule of jurisdiction fixing a definite class of questions which might be arbitrated before the stipulated court, to leave the formulation of the specific issue coming within that class for the executive.

The police power of Congress to regulate the rates on interstate commerce railroads is exercised by laying down some very general rules that rates shall be reasonable, and shall not be unduly discriminatory, and by then giving to the Interstate Commerce Commission the power under those general rules to decide what rates are unreasonable or discriminatory, and indeed to fix rates themselves.

In the argument by senators against the power of the Senate to agree that the President alone might formulate the specific agreement, much reliance was placed on the decision of the Supreme Court in Field against Clark, 145 U.S. In that case the Supreme Court merely laid down the general rule that Congress could not delegate legislative power, and then held valid a provision in the McKinley tariff act which authorized the President to apply one or another set of duties to the imports from a foreign country as he decided whether the customs laws of that country were "reciprocally unreasonable" toward us. The case, instead of helping the contention of the Senate, made strongly for the view that giving the President the power to make the specific agreement was not an unlawful delegation.

The Hay treaties of general arbitration, as I have said, excepted from the issues of a legal nature to be arbitrated "questions of national honor and vital interest." Who could tell what were not questions within these exceptions? It left a discretion in each party to insist that any question concerned its honor or vital interest. Lord Russell, when first approached as to the possibility of arbitrating the issue growing out of the Alabama claims and the mulcting of Great Britain for her failure to perform her international duties, said that she could not admit that she had ever failed in that regard, and that it was a question of national honor which she would not submit to arbitration. And yet she did, and not only did she submit it to arbitration, but she paid the judgment of $15,500,000 rendered against her by an international tribunal.

The exceptions of the Hay treaties were so broad and general that the action of the Senate in declining to allow the President to make the specific agreement under them could be strongly defended on the ground that the treaties did not sufficiently define any class of questions and therefore that the specific agreement would be the only real treaty.

A treaty of arbitration is for the purpose not only of settling disputes, but its main function is to prevent those disputes from resulting in war. A country is not likely to go to war except on an issue that involves its honor or its vital interest. Therefore, a treaty that excludes such questions from arbitration is not a treaty that covers the critical issues from which wars spring. I therefore determined, if I could, to negotiate a treaty that would leave out those exceptions and include all questions that could be arbitrated.

There are many questions between nations that concern the welfare of both, with respect to which, under any system of international justice, a nation must have absolute discretion and control of its own conduct. Take, for instance, the question whether England shall take part in our Panama Exposition. That may cause bad feeling in California or in this country generally, but no court of arbitration would make a ruling that England was obliged to take part in our exposition. That is not a justiciable question. If, however, England had agreed by treaty to take part in our exposition, then a right would be created by contract, and it would properly become the subject of arbitration and decision.

You cannot bring all subjects of difference between individuals into a municipal court. A man may be unneighborly; he may not call on his neighbor, he may notify his neighbor that he does not propose to have the latter's children come into his place; he may do a lot of unkind things that arouse the indignation of his neighbor and show he is a very mean man.

But these do not give any cause for a suit. One cannot compel his neighbor to be generous and good and courteous by a lawsuit. In other words, there is a field into which courts of justice cannot enter, whether they be municipal courts in a State, or arbitral courts between nations, and that distinction must be just as clear in an international court as in one of our domestic tribunals.

In the formulation of our treaties it was necessary to hit upon some term which would define, as a class, those causes of difference between nations that would constitute, under the principles of international law, an infringement of the legal rights of another nation analogous to rights remediable in municipal courts of justice between individuals. The description must exclude those obligations of courtesy and good-will that are enforced only by the sanction of a national conscience or by the influence of international public opinion, or by what Lord Haldane has referred to as Sittlichkeit, or international "Good Form." The analogy between matters of domestic judicial cognizance and those proper to be considered in international law tribunals is quite close. Mr. Knox found a phrase that seemed to me to be most happy in the description of the character of questions that should be arbitrated between the United States and other established governments if negotiation failed. He found it in an opinion of Chief Justice Fuller in a case in which the Supreme Court was acting as a quasi-international tribunal. One of the great examples of successful international arbitration is the arrangement for the jurisdiction of the Supreme Court under our Constitution in settling the controversies between sovereign States. It furnishes a model that in future generations will, I hope, prove to be useful in the formation of a general arbitral court for all the stable nations of the world. This case to which I refer was a controversy between Kansas and Colorado as to the water-rights of the two States and their respective residents and landowners in a stream which began in one State and ran into the other. The Chief Justice, speaking of the effect of the Constitution, said:

> Undoubtedly, as remarked by Mr. Justice Bradley in *Hans vs. Louisiana*, 134 U.S. 1, 15, the Constitution made some things justiciable, "which were not known as such at the common law; such, for example, as controversies between States as to boundary lines, and other questions admitting of judicial solution." And as the remedies resorted to by

independent States for the determination of controversies raised by collision between them were withdrawn from the States by the Constitution, a wide range of matters, susceptible of adjustment, and not purely political in their nature, was made justiciable by that instrument. 185 U.S. 125, 141.

Mr. Knox used in the treaties the word justiciable to describe the differences which the parties bound themselves to arbitrate. Those controversies only would come within the term which were just cause for reprisal by the complaining State according to international law. That law grants a reprisal only when a positive wrong has been inflicted or rights stricti juris are withheld. The rule which controls foreign and independent states in their relations to each other is that the primary and absolute right of a state is self-preservation. The improvement of her revenues, arts, agriculture, and commerce are incontrovertible rights of sovereignty. She has dominion over all things within her territory, including all bodies of water, standing or running, within her boundary-line. Her moral obligation to observe the demands of comity, that is, of good neighborly feeling, cannot be made the subject of legal controversy. In the light of such limitations fully recognized in international law, the definition of those issues intended to be arbitrated is easily applied. The language of the treaties is: "All differences . . . relating to international matters in which the high contracting parties are concerned by virtue of a claim of right made by one against the other under treaty or otherwise, and which are justiciable in their nature by reason of being susceptible of decision by the application of the principles of law or equity."

First, the differences must relate to international matters; second, they arise upon a claim of right, i.e., a right under a treaty or under principles of international law of one against the other; third, they must be justiciable, i.e., capable of judicial solution by application of the principles of law or equity. Those principles, of course, are principles of international law or equity. As this phrase is used not only in an English treaty but in a French treaty, the words are not to be confined to the technical meaning of law and equity as those words are understood in the jurisprudence of England and the United States. Still, the terms law and equity have a similar signification in many countries. Ancient systems of law grown rigid have been modified by applying more liberal principles in reaching justice. Equity has ameliorated and mitigated the severity of the law. The two words used together, therefore, were intended to comprehend all the rules of international law affecting the rights and duties of nations toward each other which are not mere rules of comity but are positive and may be properly enforced by judicial action.

The first clause of the Knox treaties provides that such questions shall be submitted to the Permanent Court of Arbitration established at The Hague, or to some other tribunal agreed to by the parties by special agreement, which shall be made on the part of the United States by the President of the United States, by and with the advice and consent of the Senate. The second clause provides for the appointment of a Joint High Commission of Inquiry to investigate any controversy between the two parties, whether within or without Article I, which investigation may be postponed for a year by either party in order to give an opportunity for negotiation and settlement. The Joint High Commission is to be constituted by each party's designating three of its own nationals to sit therein, with authority to vary the character of its appointees. The action of the Joint High Commission is to be regarded merely as advisory except in one case. If either party contends that the difference is not arbitrable by the terms of the treaty, the Joint High Commission, by a vote of five to one, may decide that it is arbitrable within the treaty, and the decision is to bind the parties. Thereafter, the arbitration is to proceed before The Hague or other tribunal as provided in the treaty. Good faith under the treaty would require, in the event of such a decision, that the President and the Senate make the specific agreement required in the first section and proceed to carry out the arbitration. Of course it would be within the power of the Senate, as, indeed, it would be within the power of the President, to decline to make such a specific agreement and thus to break their obligation and that of their government.

I suggested to Mr. Knox a form of treaty under which either party might submit to the permanent court at The Hague its complaint against the other, and the court after objection and hearing should first decide whether the complaint constituted an arbitrable case within the first clause of the section, and if it so found, it should then proceed to hear and decide the issue made. But Mr. Knox felt that the time had not arrived when so radical a proposition as that would be approved by the Senate or possibly by the country, and therefore he suggested a preliminary decision as to jurisdiction by this Joint High Commission to be composed of three Americans and three Englishmen, or three Americans and three Frenchmen, as the case might be. I regarded this as a very mild provision, because at least two Americans out of three must concur in holding that the difference in question was within the description of the general class of questions agreed to be arbitrated before the judgment could be binding on both parties. The suggestion of possible danger of injustice to the interests of the United States arising from the decision by a majority of five to one of a tribunal composed half of Americans and half of the nationals of the other treaty-making power is chimerical and imaginary.

Such objections grow out of the unwillingness of the men who suggest them to enter into any arbitration by contract or treaty in advance of the happening of the event which gives rise to the difference. Consciously or unconsciously, they are not sufficiently in favor of a judicial decision of questions between nations to be willing to lay down a general law for arbitration or to make a general classification of subjects for arbitration and abide by it. They insist on knowing all the circumstances with reference to a particular issue before they are willing to bind themselves to arbitrate it at all.

As in the consideration of the Hay treaties, so here it was argued that the President and the Senate would unlawfully delegate their treaty-making power if they agreed that a tribunal should finally adjudge that a specific difference, subsequently arising, was in the class of differences covered by the treaty. It is very difficult to argue this question because the answer to it is so plain and obvious. The question whether a specific case arising after the general treaty is made comes within the language of the treaty is a question of the construction of the treaty and its application to events subsequently arising. Construction of a treaty is the issue more frequently arbitrated between nations than any other. It is true that the question here is one of jurisdiction rather than one upon the merits of the controversy, but both arise in the construction of a treaty and both, therefore, are the normal subjects of arbitration. To leave a question arising in our foreign relations to arbitration is, of course, not a delegation of power at all. Delegated power is conferred on an agent. The tribunal does not act as agent but as a court deriving its power not from either party but from the agreement of both. The view that makes a submission to a tribunal a delegation of power to an agent would prevent the President and Senate from agreeing to arbitrate anything at all. And yet we have made arbitration treaties since the Constitution was adopted and before. The rightfulness of the power exercised under these Knox treaties to submit the question of jurisdiction to the arbitral tribunal is much clearer than was the power of the Senate to consent that the President might make the specific agreement in the Hay treaties; and this for two reasons; first, because in the Knox treaties the classification is one of clear definition as it was not in the Hay treaties; second, in the Hay treaties the President was an executive agent and the question of unlawful delegation to him alone of the treaty-making power fairly arose. But here the objection is a plain confusion of conferring power on an agent with submitting a judicial issue to a court. The only logical position that could defeat the right of the President and the Senate to agree to submit to a tribunal the question whether a subsequent difference comes within the general but definite classification of arbitrable issues in a general arbitration treaty is the utterly untenable one that the President and the Senate have no right to submit to an international tribunal at all the decision of those international matters that the President and the Senate under the Constitution are given power to deal with in our international relations.

Nevertheless, the Senate struck out the provision for a decision by the Joint High Commission. I considered this proposition the most important feature of the treaty, and I did so because I felt that we had reached a time in the making of promissory treaties of arbitration when they should mean something. The Senate halted just at the point where a possible and real obligation might be created. I do not wish to minimize the importance of general expressions of good-will and general declarations of willingness to settle everything without war, but the long list of treaties that mean but little can now hardly be made longer, for they include substantially all the countries of the world. The next step is to include something that really binds somebody in a treaty for future arbitration. The treaties of arbitration are not going to accomplish substantial progress unless we enter into them with a willingness and a consciousness that they may involve us in decisions to our detriment. We cannot win every case. Nations are like individuals; they are not always right, even though they think they are, and if arbitration is to accomplish anything, we must be willing to lose and abide by the loss. If we are to establish real arbitral courts which shall be useful as a permanent method of settling international disputes, we must agree in advance what the jurisdiction of those courts shall be, and then abide by their holding as to that jurisdiction and perform the judgments that are made against us. But if we assume that it is dangerous for us to consent to go into any arbitration, lest the court make gross errors in international law and may decide contrary to the principles of the law as we entertain them, then let us take some other method of settling international disputes.

The Senate, in its conditional concurrence in the arbitration treaties prepared by Secretary Knox, made certain reservations. The first limitation was that they should not authorize the submission to arbitration of any question affecting the admission of aliens into the United States. If there are not treaties on the subject, the rule of international law is clear and specific that no aliens can be admitted into a country without the consent of its government, and that no other nation can justly claim the right to have her nationals admitted to such territory. Why is it necessary to insert in a treaty of arbitration the principles of international law which must necessarily guide the action of an arbitral tribunal? If so, then every treaty must be an international code. But if the exception meant to exclude every question under a treaty affecting the admission of aliens, as it probably did, then it was most indefensible. If we have agreed to let in Englishmen or Frenchmen or Japanese or Chinese by treaty, on what ground ought we to evade or avoid the effect of the plighted faith of the nation to do so? Why should we be afraid to have our promises in this regard construed by an impartial tribunal? In other words, is not this a reservation of a right to violate our own plighted faith imposed by the Senate as a condition of its concurrence in the treaties? Was not the character of this condition a sufficient reason for the executive to refuse to ask the other powers to consent to it?

The second condition of exclusion is very like the first. It eliminates from arbitration any question of the admission of aliens to the educational institutions of the several States. We have made treaties in which we have agreed that the children of aliens resident in this country may enjoy the educational advantages of the children of the citizens of the States in which they live. Now, this condition was an attempt to reserve from arbitration the judgment of a high tribunal upon the question whether we should comply with our treaty obligations in that regard. Why shouldn't we? If we make the treaty, why shouldn't we fulfil it? What is the object of making a treaty if it is not to perform it? If there were not a treaty giving the right to the children of aliens to take advantage of our educational privileges, international law would impose no obligation on our government, or on the State governments either, to furnish such privileges.

The third exclusion was of any question of "the territorial integrity of the several States or of the United States." Well, suppose a question of boundary had arisen and the issue was whether land claimed by a State or the United States under a previous treaty belonged to us or belonged to the other country, why should it not be made the subject of arbitration? Didn't we arbitrate the Alaska boundary? If we have somebody else's land, if it does not belong to us and a correct construction of the treaty shows that it does not belong to us, what objection is there to our parting with it under a judgment of the court?

The fourth class of questions excluded was of the alleged indebtedness or moneyed obligation of any State of the United States. I agree that a sovereign State is not obliged to allow a suit against herself by any citizen or any individual, and that immunity from such a suit is one of the attributes of sovereignty. But the very object of international arbitrations and of general treaties to provide them is to do away with such immunity as between the parties. The commonest form of litigated questions in an international arbitration is a question of liability of a debt of one of the parties to the other.

Why should the indebtedness of the separate States be excluded in an arbitration by the United States with foreign countries? The United States is the representative of the States. Under the Constitution the United States acts for and represents the whole country, States and all. The Federal Government is the only one the other nations know. That was what our Constitution was intended to effect. If we are in favor of settling controversies between sovereignties by arbitration, in order to avoid war, the only way we can make our States parties to such arbitration is through the National Government. It is said that the United States is not liable internationally for the debts of the States. That may or may not be true, but if it is not liable, then the arbitral tribunal may say so. If it is liable in international law then it should pay the debts of the States and it would have a right of action against the States, which it might enforce because it has the right to sue a State. Why should the sovereign States of our nation be represented as complainants by our central government in arbitration and not be made defendants through the same representation? Even the Senate did not attempt to exclude debts of the United States from such arbitration. Why should the debts of the States be excluded? Of course, the treaties only affected controversies thereafter arising, so that past indebtedness was not included within their first clause. I am not at all sure that it would not be a very wholesome arrangement to fix some responsibility upon the States and to give them more motive than they have had in the past to avoid repudiation of their just obligations. The necessary exclusion of such indebtedness from questions that might be arbitrated seemed to me to be both unnecessary and improper.

The final exclusion was that the subject-matter of arbitration should not include any question dependent upon or involving the maintenance of the traditional attitude of the United States concerning American questions commonly described as the Monroe Doctrine or other purely governmental policy. John Bassett Moore, late counsellor to the Department of State, and an international lawyer of profound ability and acumen, pointed out that the Monroe Doctrine, or other governmental policy of like character, could not be made the subject of arbitration under the general clause of justiciable questions to be settled on principles of law or equity, and that no exception was necessary. I did not have the slightest objection, however, to including such a restriction in the ratification of the treaty, and, had the conditions been limited to it, I would have attempted to induce France and England to consent to it. They had consented to it in other treaties, and I presume they would have done so here. Had this been the only condition imposed by the Senate, I believe the treaties might have gone through. Senator Root and Senator Cullom urged the confirmation of the treaties with only this condition, and Senator Burton was in favor of concurring in the treaties as they were presented, and so was Senator Raynor; but Senator Lodge and Senator Bacon and the majority of the Committee on Foreign Relations took the view that in some way or other there was an unlawful delegation of the treaty-making power to a judicial tribunal appointed to construe a treaty and determine its application to particular facts.

A fair argument against the wisdom and justice of the conditions that the Senate of the United States insisted upon in its concurrence in the treaties is the fact that England and France imposed no such conditions, and their interests were just as much at stake as ours in the making and performance of the treaties. To this Senator Lodge answers that we have greatly more interests than they have to be affected by arbitration. I confess I do not understand the force of his argument. The border between Canada and ourselves is one of four thousand miles, and there are just as many legal questions affecting Canada as the United States, and the questions that affect Canada affect Great Britain. We have many questions with France and with Great Britain directly. Indeed, we have as many with them as they have with us, and, if they are willing to submit matters to arbitration, why shouldn't we?

With deference to those who oppose these treaties I must be allowed to say that the real reason for defeating them was an unwillingness to assent to the principle of arbitration without knowing something in advance of whether we were going to win or lose. That spirit is not one that will promote the cause of arbitration.

I cannot say how much good the signing of the treaties did. Had they gone through, I believe they would have been beneficial in the cause of peace. The agitation in their favor sowed some seed in the minds of the American people that may sprout and grow into useful plants; but, however this may be, those of us who believe in arbitration as the means of bringing about a general arbitral court which shall settle all issues between nations capable of judicial solution must continue the struggle, because it is right and its success will measure the progress of civilization.

I have been criticised for not going ahead with the treaty as provided by the Senate's proposed amendments, and I am quite willing to admit that there is room for discussion upon that point. I can only say why I did not. I was anxious to make a substantial step forward in the matter of arbitration treaties. I was anxious to give a model to the world of a treaty that meant something in the matter of arbitration. A treaty grid-ironed with such specific and numerous conditions as the Senate imposed, and emasculated by striking out its really binding feature, would not offer to the world such evidence of progress as to encourage the making of similar treaties between other countries. Of course, neither with England nor with France was there use for such a general arbitration treaty. It is hardly conceivable, when we consider the respective relations between the two countries and ourselves, that any difference could arise which would not be settled by arbitration. Therefore, the mere fact of making a treaty of arbitration with either had little practical or intrinsic importance upon the issues likely to arise between us and them. The treaties were important only as an encouragement to other nations in the settlement of their differences. Such a treaty, if really comprehensive, would have been thus useful and influential. As mutilated by the Senate, it seemed to me it would not effect any helpful result.

The discussion by senators of this question shows that many of them thought that such a proposition as that which I submitted to the Senate would in some way minimize the importance of the Senate in treaty making. Every senator alluded to the fact that in the constitutional convention Mr. Madison proposed that the Senate should make the treaties of the government, but that ultimately it was thought better to give the President the initiation and require a concurrence of the Senate by two thirds in treaties. Now, I am the last one to seek to minimize the importance of the Senate in either the treaty-making power or as a co-ordinate branch of the legislature. I regard the Senate as one of the most important and valuable features of the government. With the tenure of six years for each senator, with the equal representation for the large and small States, it furnishes a check against too rapid and radical action. It has served the country well in times past, and will, I doubt not, continue to be of the utmost benefit in keeping the course of our government along safely progressive lines. What ought to be done by arbitration treaties is to bind the President, the Senate, and the country to abide by the judgment of an impartial tribunal in as many cases of international difference as possible.

Mr. Bryan is now engaged in making a number of treaties which will facilitate inquiry and investigation and advisory report into differences of nations before war comes, and which are so framed as to delay hostilities though they do not provide for arbitration. I am glad that such treaties are being made. I think that the preparation of such a report will furnish useful delay while it will stimulate the negotiation of a settlement. Of course, the step is a small one, but as far as it goes it helps. The truth is that the provision with respect to the postponement of a year in the general arbitration treaties with France and Great Britain, which I have been discussing, was suggested to me by Mr. Bryan himself, though the provision for investigation and report was taken from The Hague conventions.

The ideal that I would aim at is an arbitral court in which any nation could make complaint against any other nation, and if the complaint is found by the court to be within its jurisdiction, the nation complained against should be summoned, the issue framed by pleadings, and the matter disposed of by judgment. It would, perhaps, sometimes require an international police force to carry out the judgment, but the public opinion of nations would accomplish much. With such a system we could count on a gradual abolishment of armaments and a feeling of the same kind of security that the United States and Canada have today which makes armaments and navies on our northern border entirely unnecessary.

4

Experiments in Federation for Judicial Settlement of International Disputes

The federative trend in international affairs has a distinct bearing upon the movement toward universal peace, although, of course, the federative trend has been more manifest in the formation of governments than in its effect upon the settlement of international disputes. In respect to the formation of governments this trend is the tendency, on the part of peoples under independent sovereign governments fearing foreign aggression and wishing to avoid difficulties with their neighbors, to associate themselves with their neighbors in the establishment of a common and central agency of government to which each is to delegate and convey part of its sovereignty. The control thus delegated usually covers foreign relations and the making of war and peace, and sometimes a part of the jurisdiction of internal matters. Whether the delegation of power and the structure upon which the federation is founded includes a formal means of settling differences between the members of the confederation or not, it incidentally and necessarily has this effect. We may well emphasize the importance of federation in bringing about world peace and the utility of studying the historical instances of its application as a model for a plan by which independent powers shall consent to abide the judgment in proper cases of a great, permanent, impartial international court of skilled and just judges. The subject of this chapter was suggested by Mr. Holt, the editor of The Independent and one of the strongest advocates of world peace that I know. He thought an examination of historical precedent and the application of it to the problem he has so much at heart might be useful.

The adoption of the principle of federation in political government dates far back in Grecian history. Its best example is found in the Achaian League in the Peloponnesus of Greece, which, beginning in the small territory of Achaia, gradually grew in extent of constituent cities until it included most of the Peloponnesian cities and a number of others in the northern peninsula. In its second and more perfect form, it was reorganized in 280 B. C. and lasted about one hundred and twenty-five years. It was formed for the purpose of resisting the dominion of Macedon. The members of it were independent municipal sovereignties and, in coming into the league, delegated to the executive and legislative authorities of the league, whom they chose, control over their foreign relations and the making of war and of peace. The historian Freeman finds many similarities between our Federal Constitution and that of the Achaian League. He points out the fact that Hamilton and Madison, although they studied Grecian history, were uninformed as to what he thinks the remarkable resemblance between the federal structure of government in this league and that which those statesmen did much to frame in our fundamental law of 1789. They were misled, he says, through the inaccuracies of a French historian, and instead of looking to the Achaian League, as they well might have done, they derived comfort and suggestion from erroneous accounts of the nature of the Amphictyonic League as a federal council of Greece. He points out, and other historians sustain him in the view, that the Amphictyonic League was nothing but an association of the various tribes of Greece, which, through their tribal representatives, met in a council at Delphi, where was the Oracle of Apollo, and there, in the interest of religion, adopted measures looking to its promotion and the preservation of the shrine. It was really nothing more than an ecclesiastical synod. Like not a few religious conferences, however, it occasionally adopted resolutions that touched matters that were hardly within its religious jurisdiction. It undoubtedly at times had some political influence through its religious importance. The kings of Macedon subsequently used it as an instrumentality in the politics of Greece, but it has no bearing, as Hamilton and Madison thought it did, upon the use of the federative principle in the formation of governments. Mr. Freeman says: "It is clear that Hamilton and Madison knew hardly anything more of Grecian history than what they had picked from the 'Observations' of the Abbé Mably. But it is no less clear that they were incomparably better qualified to understand and apply what they did know."

The constitution of the Achaian League did not provide for a federal tribunal, and I cannot find in the somewhat lengthy volume of Mr. Freeman any reference whatever to judicial matters in the history of federation in Greece and Rome. Mr. Freeman says that it was the custom among Grecian cities, when the international rights of one were broken by another, to submit the issue to the arbitrament of a third city. Probably in this way the differences between the members of the Achaian Federation were settled when they arose. But it is a thing that we must realize, though it is a little hard to do so, that courts and judges as such—having only judicial functions—are a comparatively modern invention. The Book of Judges in the Old Testament suggests the idea that they must have had judges in Israel, but while these judges heard judicial controversies, as we know, they were really civil patriarchal rulers who exercised executive and legislative as well as judicial powers.

Even in the golden era of the Roman Empire, when the rule of law was being established by law-writers and jurisconsults, in the four centuries before the Code of Justinian, there were no judges as such. There was an executive officer, called the Prætor, whose business it was to execute the law. He was not generally a lawyer. When he had a case in the execution of the law that involved a judicial inquiry he formulated his case and submitted it to a referee, who was not necessarily a jurisconsult or learned in the law. He was called a Judex, and from the title given him we get the name of judge. The Prætor was elected every year, so that, in spite of the great debt that we owe to republican and imperial Rome for the supremacy that they gave to law and its administration and the symmetry that they gave to jurisprudence, we cannot say that we owe to them a judicial system of permanent, learned, and independent courts. For that we must look to the history of Anglo-Saxon civil liberty, because it is in English history that we find the ultimate division of governmental functions between the executive and legislative on the one hand and the judicial on the other. The term "court" is a late word derived from the fact that the hearing of the tribunal was heard in a court or courtyard. This failure to recognize a difference between the executive, legislative, and judicial functions manifests itself even now when we come to consider international relations and tribunals for the settlement of international disputes. I shall refer to this later. After the ancient local proprietary or manorial courts lost their jurisdiction, the King of England in council or in Parliament became the seat of all governmental power, executive, legislative, and judicial. Parliament was not only a legislative body but it was a court. Lords and Commons met originally in one body. Now the two bodies are separated; the judicial function is still exercised by the House of Lords. The King sat in his own court, which gave it the name of "King's Court." Edward IV was the last king to do so in person. Then the King delegated this judicial duty to his justiciaries, who held the King's Court, and attended the King wherever he went. This caused great inconvenience in private cases, and, finally, in the Magna Charta that was extorted from King John by the Barons at Runnymede, that monarch agreed that the assizes should be held at certain times in every county of his realm by his judges, so that individuals might not be put to the trouble of following the King about in his travels in order to get justice. The use which the Stuart kings made of the judges to sustain their arbitrary course led to a change in their tenure after the revolution of 1688 and the Bill of Rights, so that early in the reign of Queen Anne they ceased to hold office at the pleasure or during the life of the King and became judges for life and independent of his control. We have thus inherited our conception that a court is a body that decides cases according to the law and the fact, without influence by the executive or even the legislative power except as the legislature enacts positive law and the court construes and enforces it as a uniform rule of conduct.

No such idea of a judicial tribunal, set apart and independent, prevailed either in Greece or in Rome, or during the Middle Ages, or during the Holy Roman Empire. It is a later conception in continental countries. But it is most important that this idea of absolute justice and of having judges who in giving judgment are impartial and independent of political policy or legislative direction, should be recognized in our international relations.

It is true that the Progressive party and its leaders are now seeking to destroy this conception, to take away the independence of the judiciary, to remove the idea of absolute justice which the independence of the judiciary is supposed to secure, and to mingle in its administration of specific cases the desire of the sovereign electorate. Heretofore we have thought that in tracing back the history of our liberties from Magna Charta through the Petition of Right and the Bill of Rights, the Declaration of Independence, which itself insists on the independence of the judiciary, and the Federal Constitution we have had something to be grateful for in the judicial system which we have inherited. This seems a far cry from the Achaian League and the federative trend of government, but I think I can make it seem relevant before I get through.

We find in the Grecian example the fact that men began to realize that while a Grecian city was capable of furnishing a useful and happiness-giving government, yet when it came to resist the aggressions of a stronger neighbor the people of the city must look for aid among those who were similarly circumstanced and yield something of their sovereignties to one joint federal authority for their protection. There have been in history since that time many instances of federations. The Holy Roman Empire, theoretically and in the sonorous titles of the Emperor, began with Julius Cæsar and lasted until Napoleon's time. It presented at stages in its history an important phase of the federative principle for our present use. After the breaking up of the real Roman Empire by many different barbarian invasions and migrations, and after the nationalizing spirit became stronger and before the Holy Roman Empire lost all its power, there were heated discussions as to the relation of the Emperor to the government of men. The prevailing theory was that all secular government came from God through the people to the Emperor, and while kingdoms and dukedoms and principalities and the electorates whose chiefs elected the Emperor exercised independent government in their respective jurisdictions, they all seemed theoretically to concede their subordination to the divine right of the Emperor in secular government. He was called the Emperor of Peace, and one of his recognized duties and powers was to keep the kings and

dukes and other potentates who were under him from war. He was generally unsuccessful, but the high character of this duty on his part and the
conception which the statement of the duty showed to be in the minds of
men are interesting and significant. While it cannot be said that the Holy
Roman Empire was the result of a federation, because in theory the Emperor created Kings and princes, nevertheless, as national life developed
into different sovereignties, the only relation that they had to the Emperor
was a result akin to what would have happened had they been separate
entities and had then united in a federation for purposes that the maintenance of the imperial power continued to serve. Mr. Bryce, in his history
of the Holy Roman Empire, speaking of this feature of the empire, says:

> With feudal rights no longer enforceable, and removed, except in his
> patrimonial lands, from direct contact with the subject, the Emperor
> was not, as heretofore, conspicuously a German and a feudal king, and
> occupied an ideal position less marred by the incongruous accidents of
> birth and training, of national and dynastic interests.
>
> To that position three cardinal duties were attached. He who held it
> must typify spiritual unity, must preserve peace, must be a fountain of
> that by which alone among imperfect men peace is preserved and re-
> stored—law and justice. . . . And he was, therefore, above all things,
> claiming, indeed, to be upon earth the representative of the Prince of
> Peace, bound to listen to complaints and to redress the injuries inflicted
> by sovereigns or peoples upon each other; to punish offenders against
> the public order of Christendom; to maintain through the world, look-
> ing down as from a serene height upon the schemes and quarrels of
> meaner potentates, that supreme good without which neither arts or
> letters, nor the gentler virtues of life, can rise and flourish. The mediae-
> val empire was in its essence what its modern imitators have sometimes
> professed themselves—the Empire of Peace; the oldest and noblest title
> of its head was "Imperator pacificus." And, that he might be the peace-
> maker, he must be the expounder of justice and the author of its con-
> crete embodiment, positive law; chief legislator and supreme judge of
> appeal, like his predecessor, the compiler of the Corpus Juris, the one
> and only source of all legitimate authority.

The result of this view of the position of the Holy Roman Empire in
the Middle Ages and later on is seen in a number of conceptions published

in those dark centuries. They are referred to by Mr. Thomas Willing Balch in a paper on *The Advance of International Peace through Legal and Judicial Means,* which he read at the 1912 meeting of the Society for the Judicial Settlement of International Disputes at Washington. In 1306 a French barrister, Pierre DuBois, in a treatise entitled *De Recuperatione Terre Sancte,* urged that the Catholic states of Europe should form an alliance, with the King of France at their head, in order to secure peace among themselves. Should trouble arise between any members of the proposed alliance, DuBois urged that their difference be settled by a quasi-court appointed *ad hoc* and composed of six members, and consisting of three ecclesiastics and "three others from both parties." In each case the Pope was to be appealed to to review the decision. In 1461 King Podiebrad of Bohemia, adopting the plans of Antoine Marini, his chancellor, negotiated with other sovereigns for the establishment of a federal state which was to have a federal congress composed of ambassadors to sit at Bâle. And Henry IV proposed, at the suggestion of his minister, the Duke of Sully, what was called the Great Design. Though this was in the form of a federation to avoid war, it was said to be not a genuine proposal of universal peace but a plan to give France the leadership of Europe. Nevertheless, it seems to have suggested a good many real plans for the accomplishment of its avowed purpose. In 1623 a Parisian monk, Emeric Cruce, proposed that all sovereignties of the world should send ambassadors to some city like Venice, and that when two sovereign powers disagreed, the ambassadors should plead the cause of their respective sovereigns before the other assembled ambassadors, who should decide the issue, and the judgment was to be enforced by the combined power of the sovereignties represented in the court. Within two years after the publication of this plan, Grotius, in his epoch-making work on the *Law of War and Peace,* urged upon sovereigns the convening of congresses for peaceable settlement of international disputes.

For our purpose, perhaps, the most interesting instance of federation other than that of our own country was the Swiss Republic. This federation is remarkable in that it was organized in the thirteenth century and has continued until today. It illustrates a continuous union of people who speak three different languages, in the very centre of Europe, and therefore in the centre of a continental battle-ground. It was doubtless the result of the same desire for protection against foreign aggression that prompted the Achaian League, but it lasted longer. While the Swiss people differ in language they resemble each other in character, and there was a national spirit among them, early developed, that insisted on local self-government but on united action against invaders. Doctor Scott, in an interesting address before the last annual meeting of the Society for the Judicial Settlement of International Disputes, invited attention to the precedent of the Swiss Republic in the development of the federation principle into a national court after centuries of association, and he quotes the following from M. Lardy, a Swiss diplomat, who presided in an arbitration between Russia and Turkey, 1911:

> Is it improper for me to state that more than six centuries have passed since the first of August, 1291, when the Swiss burghers signed their first treaty of alliance on the shore of the Lake of the Four Cantons, at the foot of our snow-clad Alps? On that memorable day which the Swiss people annually celebrate with bonfires on every mountain top, while all the church-bells call upon the Almighty to protect the Fatherland, the Confederate Cantons made an arbitral pact with each other, binding themselves to submit their differences to the more prudent inhabitants (prudentiores) of their valleys and creating the force needed to assure the execution of the award. For centuries Switzerland developed under the protection of arbitration, until the day came when it was enabled to commit to its federal tribunal the decision of a large number of disputes of a public nature and to intrust the rights and liberties of its citizens to the federal tribunal. Will the court of The Hague some day become the federal tribunal of the nations? In Switzerland, small as it is, centuries were required to create a permanent federal tribunal and to secure its acceptance by public opinion. It is the part of wisdom to believe that many years must elapse before the basis of an agreement be found which will assure the independence of the various states and guarantee the moral heritage of every people in the universal concert of nations.

It is remarkable that this system of arbitration, begun six hundred years ago, did not develop into a federal Supreme Court until 1845. We may sincerely hope that it will not take six centuries for the court of arbitration, established at the first Hague Conference, to develop into the arbitral court proposed in the second Hague Conference.

The next federation in point of time for our consideration is that which we of the United States have offered as a model to the world. I pass it by, for the present, to come to some more recent. We find in the relation of the Privy Council of England to three great governments that are an important part of the British Empire, instances of the trend toward a federal court whose authority and whose function are closely akin to what an international court should exercise. I refer to Canada, Australia, and South Africa. The compromises that were made and the statesmanship and patriotism that were shown in reaching an agreement for federation of the great English and French provinces in one Dominion of Canada, owning a half continent and containing now eight millions of people, form a notable history that parallels the struggle our ancestors made to frame and ratify our Constitution. Indeed, the framers of the Canadian federation profited much by the lessons from our history. The same thing is true of the formation of the Australian federation, with five millions of people, which in some respects more resembles ours than does Canada. The South African federation, the last one formed, under the British Empire, has less of the federative principle and more of the direct government than either of the other two, or of our own.

But in all these federations there is a Supreme Court which has the power of settling the questions arising under federation law and determining the questions which may arise between the members of the federation. In each, these members are great states quite like our own, but called provinces in Canada, which carry on their local self-governments and exercise an autonomy differing somewhat from that exercised by our States, but all illustrating, in a most satisfactory way, the value of the federative principle, by which the idiosyncrasies of locality and local tradition are given full scope in the provincial governments, while the general law of the federation, as a whole, is left to the federative parliament, courts, and executive to prescribe, interpret, and execute. Each has a supreme court which passes on the quasi-international relations between the members that go to make up the federation. And then what is even more important and more significant of the possibilities of a world federation is the judicial appeal that may be taken from the supreme courts of these Federations to the Privy Council sitting in England that acts as a supreme tribunal for all the quasi-independent governments of the entire empire. Sir Charles Fitzpatrick, the Chief Justice of Canada, has been invited to sit in the Privy Council in the coming summer in a cause concerning the boundary between Newfoundland (which is a separate colony of Great Britain) and the Dominion of Canada. In the decision of such a case it is inevitable that the high tribunal will administer the general principles of international law.

Coming now to our own government and its organization, it is entirely unnecessary for me to go into the general history of the organization of the original federation, the history of the adoption of the Articles of Confederation after the Declaration of Independence, or the organization of our government under our present Constitution into a more compact union, making us a nation before the world.

Under the Articles of Confederation, Congress was made the tribunal to settle controversies and differences arising between the independent sovereign States that made up the Confederation. The name "Congress" indicated the character of the body. Congress, in the language of diplomacy, was a term applied to a meeting of sovereigns or of their ambassadors for international action. Congress under the Federation was called upon to settle at least one State controversy. That was the dispute between Pennsylvania and Connecticut as to the title of lands in the Wyoming Valley now in Pennsylvania. Congress selected from the different States a list of men from whom the parties were enabled to select a certain number to constitute the court. The court sat at Trenton, heard evidence for forty days, and decided the controversy in favor of Pennsylvania, and in this judgment the State of Connecticut acquiesced.

In the Constitution of 1789 the judicial power of the United States was extended to controversies between two States and between a State and a foreign state. And these controversies were to be heard as original cases before the Supreme Court. The Constitution also extended the judicial power of the United States to any suit in which the United States was a party. This enables the United States to sue any State, and the fact that the State is a party gives original jurisdiction to the Supreme Court to consider the cause. One such case has been tried growing out of a dispute in a boundary that involved the title of the State of Texas to Greer County. The question was whether Greer County belonged to the United States or whether it was a part of Texas. The Supreme Court heard the case and decided in favor of the United States, and Greer County subsequently became part of the new State of Oklahoma. It is unnecessary to enumerate the number of cases in which the Supreme Court has been called upon to adjudicate between the sovereign States and to enforce international law in their controversies. Mr. Wickersham, when attorney-general, reviewed them at length in an interesting paper read by him before the 1912 meeting of the Society for Judicial Settlement of International Disputes. In my last chapter I referred to the case of *Kansas vs. Colorado,* 185 U.S. 146, from the language of Chief Justice Fuller's opinion in which the term "justiciable" suggested its use in the general arbitration treaties to describe the kind of controversies which might properly be arbitrated. In that case the chief justice said: "Sitting, as it were, as an international as well as a domestic tribunal, we apply federal law, State law, and international law, as the exigencies of the particular case may demand."

In the same case, reported again in 206 U.S. 46, 97, Mr. Justice Brewer, delivering the opinion of the court, says:

> As Congress cannot make compacts between the States, as it cannot, in respect to certain matters, by legislation compel their separate action, disputes between them must be settled either by force or else by appeal to tribunals empowered to determine the right and wrong thereof. Force, under our system of government, is eliminated. The clear language of the Constitution vests in this court the power to settle those disputes. We have exercised that power in a variety of instances, determining in the several instances the justice of the dispute. Nor is our jurisdiction ousted even if, because Kansas and Colorado are States sovereign and independent in local matters, the relations between them depend in any respect upon principles of international law. International law is no alien in this tribunal. In the Paquete Habana, 175 U.S. 677, 700, Mr. Justice Gray declared: "International law is part of our law, and must be ascertained and administered by the courts of justice of appropriate jurisdiction as often as questions of right depending upon it are duly presented for their determination."

Mr. Wickersham calls attention to the fact that very few instances have occurred in which a foreign state has availed itself of the privilege of suing a State of the United States in the Supreme Court, but he notes a case in which I had the honor to be of counsel, entitled "In re Cooper," 138 U.S. 404, in which, with the knowledge and approval of the Imperial Government of Great Britain and in the name of the attorney-general for the Dominion of Canada, an application was made to the Supreme Court to issue a writ of prohibition to prevent an admiralty court in Alaska from selling under a decree of forfeiture a Canadian schooner for alleged violation of the statute of the United States against pelagic sealing, on the ground that this sealing was done beyond the jurisdiction of the government of the United States in the open seas. This was a very emphatic testimonial to the confidence which the British Government had in our Supreme Court, and the chief justice acknowledged it in the following language:

> In this case—Her Britannic Majesty's attorney-general of Canada has presented, with the knowledge and approval of the imperial Government of Great Britain, a suggestion on behalf of the claimant. He represents no property interest in the vessel, as is sometimes done by consuls, but only a public political interest. We are not insensible to the courtesy implied in the willingness thus manifested that this court should proceed to a decision on the main question argued for the petitioner; nor do we permit ourselves to doubt that under such circumstances the decision would receive all the consideration that the utmost good faith would require; but it is very clear that, presented as a political question merely, it would not fall within our province to determine it. We allude to this in passing, but not at all with the intention of indicating that the suggestion itself diminishes the private rights of the claimant in any degree. (143 U.S. 503)

This international recognition of our own Federal court brings us to the larger projects for world federation for judicial purposes which centre in The Hague.

The federation in international matters took definite form in the invitation issued by the Emperor of Russia to hold the First Hague Conference. At that conference an agreement was entered into by the many nations that took part in it, embracing all the important nations of the world, providing a so-called permanent court of arbitration for the settlement of international disputes. In a strict sense it is not permanent, nor is it a court. The agreement does invite each one of the signatory powers to furnish a list of competent persons from whom parties seeking the form of procedure provided may select arbitrators. But it might better be called a permanent plan and form of procedure for temporary arbitrations in the settlement of international disputes.

The Second Conference, however, made a great advance over this. It adopted a form for a permanent international prize court and framed a definite organization of that court. It provided that the judges appointed by the following contracting parties, Germany, the United States of America, Austria, France, Great Britain, Italy, Japan, and Russia, should always be summoned to sit, while judges appointed by the other contracting powers should sit in rotation as shown in the table annexed to the convention, and the same judge might be appointed by several of the powers. It provided for an appeal from the existing prize courts of any nation to this international prize court and bound the powers to abide by the result of the appeal. Of course, services of a prize court are called into requisition only during naval warfare. The prize jurisdiction is part of the system of legal piracy that continues to be recognized as within civilized warfare, by which private property of the citizens of an enemy, carried in trading vessels under the flag of the enemy, though harmless and unarmed, nevertheless may be captured as lawful prize and sold for the benefit of the officers and men of the capturing war-vessel. By the present rules of naval warfare, the prize has to be taken into a port of the country of the capturer, and there, in a proceeding before an admiralty court sitting as a prize court, the vessel and her cargo are adjudged lawful prize and sold and the proceeds distributed. It was impossible under our Constitution for us to agree to an appeal from the decision of our prize courts, whether district or supreme, to an international prize court, but instead of that we agreed to have the cause submitted to the international prize court, and if the decision of the Supreme Court or the local court was found to be wrong, to allow the international prize court to adjudge damages against the United States sufficient to compensate the person injured by the decision. Such a procedure had been foreshadowed in several cases in which the judgments of the Supreme Court in prize appeals had been held to be erroneous by an international arbitration, and an award on the basis of the arbitration had been made and paid by Congress. The international-prize-court provisions, although agreed upon in detail at The Hague Conference, have not been embodied in a convention between the powers because of a difficulty in settling what the law of prize is. In order to do this, a conference of the powers assembled in London and agreed to what was known as the Declaration of London, formulating a code of rules regulating the rights of neutrals and belligerents with respect to neutral commerce. I am sorry to say that England has not consented to that declaration, and her failure to do so has thus far made impossible the consummation of the very noteworthy plan for an international court of prize.

But the international court of prize is important not for itself but because of what has grown out of it, to wit, the recommendation of the Second Conference of The Hague that we shall have an arbitral court of justice permanent in its membership, with paid members, who shall take no part except as judges in any international dispute. This has failed of complete concurrence by all the powers interested, because every power wished to have a judge on this court, and, as there are forty-six signatory powers, such a court is impossible. Why they might not make the same arrangement that was made in the international prize court as to membership, is not quite clear. Probably a good many of the powers were not interested in naval warfare, and therefore not in the decisions of an international prize court, while they might be in the decisions of an international court of more general jurisdiction.

The recommendation of this Second Hague Conference of both courts, however, is most gratifying, and if followed will constitute a long step forward in the mode of settling international disputes, closely approximating that of settling controversies in our domestic tribunals. Attention has been called by a number of persons who have followed closely international arbitration, and who well understand municipal judicial systems, notably Mr. Knox and Mr. Root, to the difference between international arbitration as it has been practised and the result of the submission of causes to a domestic court. The tribunal of arbitration has usually been composed of representatives from each party and an umpire or umpires from other countries. The decision resulting has too often been not a clean judgment of the facts and the law on the merits, but it has been a compromise with the hope that each party may acquiesce in the suggestion of settlement. It is really a continuation of diplomatic effort to reach a settlement satisfactory to both parties with as much gentle pressure as may be. The presence on the court of representatives of each party is calculated to bring about such a result. They fall into the attitude not of judges but of partisan claimants in the consultations of the tribunal; and apparently it is not expected that they will ever consent, or make themselves parties, to a judgment adverse to the serious claims of the country which they are supposed to represent. I do not think it is too much to say that this has generally been the continental view. With English and American jurists seated on the tribunal, exceptions have been known. They have generally approached questions presented to them as members of a tribunal in the same way in which they would approach questions presented to them as judges in a municipal court. Thus, in the issue between Great Britain and the United States as to the Alaskan boundary, Lord Chief Justice Alverston sat as one of the arbitrators and voted to decide the main question in favor of the United States. His attitude was very severely criticised, but he justified himself as an English judge, and said if he was to be selected as a judge, he expected to act as a judge. So, in the seals controversy, Mr. Justice Harlan, while concurring in the claim of the United States in one aspect, voted to reject the claim of territorial jurisdiction made on behalf of the United States and earlier set forth at great length by Mr. Blaine when secretary of state.

But it may be asked why this method of compromise in arbitrations is not the best way of settling international disputes. Does it not prevent the feeling of bitterness that more drastic judgments might create in the minds of the defeated nations and thus will promote peace and good-will? I think not. A nation which has a good cause, or thinks it has, will hesitate to submit the cause to a tribunal that will in practice and by custom abate part of the claim, not on grounds of justice, but in order to satisfy the natural partisan feeling of the opposing party. It is a fearless, clear-headed, justice-loving court that will command the confidence of the nations and will induce the submission of claims to it. A permanent international court sitting with a permanent membership, and hearing case after case, will acquire not only a facility of decision but also will acquire the joint judicial spirit in approaching all kinds of questions. We cannot expect that in the beginning we shall have perfect results. We must anticipate the presence of prejudice in the court, but the longer that it exists and the more cases it has to decide and the more its decisions form a consistent system of law, the more confident may we be that it will grow into a great court for the consideration of international questions having the respect of the civilized world.

The independence of the English and American judiciary has created—I think it may be said without invidious distinction—a higher standard of judicial impartiality because of the historical growth of our courts into their present attitude than prevails in any other countries, and, therefore, even in a case between England and the United States, I would quite as willingly submit the case to three English judges and two American judges sitting in a court of five as I would to a court consisting wholly of jurists from other countries.

It is very clear that if we can secure any system for a permanent court which shall sit to hear such cases as are presented to it, the number of cases which will be submitted and the decisions arising therefrom will be of sufficient influence to induce the submission of more and more cases to such an impartial tribunal as it will prove to be. The formation of the court is a most important step, because, with the cases that are submitted to it, it will become an object-lesson. Time and time again the situation will arise when a government by public opinion of the world will be forced into some other method than defiant refusal to meet an equitable claim, and then, when such a court exists, it will propose submission to it of the pending question in order to escape from a more embarrassing solution.

With the formation of The Hague Court of Arbitral Justice, as recommended by the Second Hague Conference, for the consideration of all questions arising between the nations of the world, I shall look forward with confident hope to the signing within a few decades, or a half-century (for what is such a period in the achievement of such a triumph of righteousness?), of a general treaty or convention by all the great powers, in which they shall agree to submit all justiciable controversies to this tribunal. I hope that they will make the convention in the form of a federal agreement by which this court shall be recognized as a federal court, with the right on the part of any nation aggrieved against another nation to bring its complaint into the court, have the court determine its jurisdiction of the complaint in accord with the definition of its jurisdiction in the convention, and then summon the offending nation and require an answer, and after hearing enter judgment. Why do I hope for this? Am I overenthusiastic? It may take time, I admit, but not so many years as scoffers suppose.

The usefulness of examining history with reference to the federative trend of government is to show that federation is a normal and natural method of taking care of and settling, in an effective way, justiciable questions between sovereignties. The theoretical power and duty of adjustment of differences between nations by the Holy Roman Empire induced great conceptions such as I have described at a time when war was a normal condition between nations and peace was the exception. It was such a conception that led to the urgent recommendation of that great international lawgiver, Grotius. The growth of arbitration into a federal court in the history of the Swiss Republic is another instance of the natural development from independence into federation, and then from negotiation and arbitration into a federal court for settling differences between the federated sovereignties. The international jurisdiction of the Supreme Court of the United States is another most significant model and points the natural historical way of settling international disputes both in theory and in practice. The federative principle in the organization of the three great English federations, Canada, Australia, and South Africa, the establishment of a supreme court in each federation to decide between the members, and the real character of the Privy Council in England in settling the judicial questions between members of the British Empire, all point more and more nearly to the goal we seek of a world federation court.

But it is said: "If this federative trend of government has existed since Grecian times, and was recognized in the Middle Ages, in the days of Charlemagne and Henry the Fowler and Frederick Barbarossa, why has it failed in the long time which has elapsed since then to develop into the court you seek? Why may you expect now more rapid progress after centuries of delay?" One reason is the success of the use of federal courts in settling differences really inter-sovereign, if I may coin a word, as seen in these modern federal governments, and a further reason is that the whole world is aroused to the advantage of peace, as it never has been before. Nations of the world are growing closer and closer to each other. Facility of transportation and facility of communication have developed a knowledge and an interest among the people of one country in the doings of the people of another that was never known before. We follow with close attention the Ulster controversy, the political tragedy in France, the trial involving the military conduct of army officers in Alsace, the Jewish persecution in Russia, the parliamentary proceedings in China, the overthrow of a party in the responsible parliamentary government of Japan. We may be sure that peoples of other countries, with equal facility, follow the important events in this country. Money is being poured into the coffers of our missionary societies for the purpose of promoting Christian civilization throughout the Orient and in Africa to give us in those countries advance agents and pioneers representing altruism and the promotion of true religion. The united spirit of search for truth and the promotion of world brotherhood shown in the universities the world over, and the gradual forming of a world public opinion, of higher moral standards, all create an atmosphere in which we may be sure this federative trend in international matters will be fostered and encouraged to extend to the creation of a federal world court whose judgments nations will ultimately regard as binding in the same sense as those which domestic courts render.

But the query is made: "How will judgments of such a court be enforced; what will be the sanction for their execution?" I am very little concerned about that. After we have gotten the cases into court and decided and the judgments embodied in a solemn declaration of a court thus established, few nations will care to face the condemnation of international public opinion and disobey the judgment. When a judgment of that court is defied, it will be time enough to devise methods to prevent the recurrence of such an international breach of faith.

Undoubtedly when such a court is established, and a series of judgments have been delivered, these will constitute great and valuable additions to international law. The controversies will invite application of recognized principles to new facts, and the variation that new applications will involve will widen the law, and the court will be an authoritative source for its growth and development. It will be judge-made law, and the growth of the international law will be as the common law has grown, adapting itself to new conditions and expanding on principles of morality and general equity.

It is, therefore, federation to the extent of a permanent international court that offers the solution of the problem of how to escape war, how to induce nations to give up the burden of armaments, and how to broaden and make certain our system of international law. It will be natural with a court thus established, and with the closer union that it will necessarily bring between the various powers of the earth, that congresses of nations shall be called at convenient periods, in which, by treaties, an international code may be adopted to meet the defects in accepted international law which the issues and judgments in the arbitral court may develop, and which the judicial discretion of such a tribunal may not be broad enough to supply. Such a court and such a code will greatly promote justice in the world and the peace of nations.